3,75

FREEDOM FROM STRESS

FREEDOM

FROM

STRESS

ERNEST HOLMES

Compiled and Edited by
WILLIS KINNEAR

SCIENCE OF MIND PUBLICATIONS
Los Angeles, California

SEVENTH PRINTING – JUNE 1980

Published by SCIENCE OF MIND PUBLICATIONS
3251 West Sixth Street, Los Angeles, California 90020

CONTENTS

FOREWORD

In the series of Annual Editions of *Science of Mind* Magazine this is the fourth volume containing the miscellaneous writings of Ernest Holmes.

This valuable material first appeared many years ago in the magazine, but copies of those earlier issues are no longer available. The dynamic quality of his ideas are of a timeless nature and need availability and permanency in a publication such as this.

Although he was considered a profound thinker and a great religious philosopher, Dr. Holmes was at the same time a very practical man. He felt that abstract theory was a needed foundation, but unless and until it could be brought down to earth and applied to produce demonstrable results in one's experience, it was of little value.

The material this volume contains emphasizes the necessity of facing the facts of life, but at the same time the need to resolve the problems of living through the recognition and application of spiritual concepts.

The ideas to be found in these pages are specific, they are concise and simple. They are applicable in the correcting and reconstructing of your life so that it may embody more health and happiness, more success and security.

Science of Mind Publications

INTRODUCTION

Most people feel that life is a continual struggle and that they are always on the losing side. Everything and everybody is against them and the stresses and strains of just being alive are almost more than they can endure.

Such feelings arise from efforts to control their environment, conflicts with others, and an apparent inability to get along even with themselves. There is a tendency to think that these problems are peculiar to this era, but actually they have been with man since the dawn of consciousness and awareness of the world around him.

Our tensions take many forms and involve such emotions as fear, guilt, anxiety, and hate. Accompanying them are their physically damaging effects which result in illnesses.

It has been shown that unless we were kept alive and awake by a certain amount of stress we would just vegetate. The problem is to discover the level at which we best function and not let extreme reactions so envelop us that we literally let the matter of living get the better of us. Not only do we want to live, but we want to enjoy the best life has to offer.

We need not so much to avoid the eternal problems of living but rather to adequately meet and control them by controlling and directing our internal responses. It is only as we gather our mental resources that we may guide and direct ourselves, and in so doing bring to bear on the stress-producing situations the only force by which man has ever been able to achieve and progress — the power of his own thought.

We all desire and need freedom from damaging pressures in whatever form they may be affecting us. We cannot escape from living but we can learn how to live; what living means, what is involved, and how to use the power of Life within us. Only then may we discover the path that leads from the limiting and disastrous bondage of stress to a new life that embodies health, happiness, and success.

It is hoped that the pages of this book will enable you to do for yourself what no one else can do for you — discover the freedom and the joy of living you desire.

W. K.

PROLOGUE

The power of life is in our own consciousness. We must turn there and re-create our environment after the image of harmony instead of discord. It is not enough just to believe that it can be done. We all know, in some degree, that it can be done. But it is not enough just to say these things are so; we must prove them. There must be a continuous betterment in our affairs, in everything we touch, if we are going to prove that we know what we are talking about.

We must believe that God *is*. Our belief in God must be clearer than our belief in evil. Peace must destroy the illusion of fear, and faith must overcome doubt. All of our affairs are but thoughts cast upon the screen of experience as temporary events. In the silence of our own soul we walk back and back, turning away from the apparent condition until, finally, we emerge in the broader field where we are unified with the one Source of all things.

Every man can do this, and the Almighty has already given us the power. We shall never know that it actually works until we do it, but once we have done it there is added to our lives and experiences a something which will so change us that we shall never again be the same; our whole reaction to life will forever-more be different. We shall have made one definite step in our spiritual evolution.

— *Ernest Holmes*

PART ONE

NEW HORIZONS OF THINKING

To adequately meet or solve any problem which may confront you there is first the necessity to discover what it is you have to work with. Your immediate reaction is to search for external things to be used. Often externals can be of great value, but you have to go a step farther than this; namely, you have to initially discover the nature of that which uses other things — yourself.

When you say you are overwhelmed by excessive stress, what do you mean when you refer to yourself? Just what is the individual that reacts, that has feelings, that thinks?

It thus becomes necessary that you try to determine who and what you are before you can find out the nature, the quality, and the power of the tools you have to work with. There is that within you which, properly recognized and applied, may enable you to open up new horizons of your thought. It is only as you learn about yourself that you may learn to create a life more to your liking.

1

REDISCOVER YOURSELF

"Know Thyself"

After having passed through an age of scientism, when people were afraid of being thought fools unless they could give what seemed like logical answers to everything, we are now witnessing a strange phenomenon in the evolution of thought. Many of our leading scientific minds, having apparently analyzed the material universe to a vanishing point, are now beginning to consider that the spiritual and the mental realms are fundamental realities. Marvelous as the previous age has been, its material frontier is falling into a state of collapse.

The objective world has pushed forward as far as it can go without encountering the invisible domain, and we are entering a period of discovery on this new frontier which will neither collapse nor exhaust itself. The farther out we push the horizon of mind, the more we are delving into the nature of man. Instead of coming to the end of a road, we continue to arrive at new points of expansion. The more we learn the more we find there is left to be discovered.

That which psychology analyzes is but a fragment of the real man. The search for the real man involves a peering through the objective and subjective into a universal height, depth, and breadth; a delving, not only into the real nature of man, but into the nature of Reality Itself. If we hope to arrive at any real understanding of the nature of ourselves, we must try to ascertain our Source.

We know a little about our physiological nature; we know less about our psychological nature; we know almost nothing about our mental nature. Our spiritual nature is so hidden that it is revealed only in dots and dashes, only in infrequent flashes of consciousness, brief flashes when men cease to be men and become as gods, temporarily. There is no doubt about the power such men have displayed, because if any man could push beyond the ordinary laws of cause and effect and his limited understanding of them, just in one moment's thought, then his Divine nature would be released through him by an immutable Law. A man could not attain such a use of spiritual Power unless he had first harmonized himself with Reality to such a degree that it would be impossible for him to use this Power destructively. He would have to use It for beneficent purposes only. While it seems certain that all thought has some power, it is equally certain that we arrive at the most powerful use of thought only through constructive methods. The Universe cannot be divided against Itself.

Man has a nature beyond the merely psychological. He has an at-one-ment with the Spirit. The merely psychological or mental activity may or may not be constructive, but spiritual Power can never be used negatively. At all times we must carefully differentiate between mental deception and spiritual illumination. In cases of spiritual illumination there must have been opened up a broader something which, as it were, swallowed up the littleness of man and gave to the world the greater hope it has had, and to religion its vitality. For it is not the negative but the affirmative side of religions which has caused them to endure throughout the ages. Nothing can be of the nature of God unless it is good. Nothing can be good which seeks to harm anyone.

For the first time in the history of human thought we are coming to a place where intelligent people are setting about to rediscover man. People are becoming afraid of what the intellect, uncontrolled by spiritual ideals, may do to the human race. The

11

intellect has produced such terrible instruments of warfare that the world contemplates another international conflict as race suicide and the closing chapter of our present civilization. Man is falling back aghast at the thought of his own self-destruction and is searching anew for a deeper spiritual meaning to life. Many modern scientific men are showing great earnestness in an endeavor to find something that gives value to life other than the mere uncovering and use of the mechanical operations of energy. Too much knowledge with too little wisdom is dangerous.

Many modern scientific people are taking a very sincere position when they humble themselves intellectually by declaring that perhaps, after all, Spirit *is* a reality. The need of the world is to have spiritual values given back to it. The spiritual man must be uncovered, rediscovered. We must again return to the pathway of faith.

The world is on the eve of the greatest spiritual revival it has ever had, not a revival of religious convictions so much as a renewed awareness of spiritual realities. Our particular beliefs are all right because they are individual, and it is right and proper that each should spread his own table with the type of spiritual food which pleases his intellectual and emotional appetite. It is right that each should be nourished by his own belief, but it is first necessary that his personal belief should be imbedded in a logical concept of eternal Reality.

Back of the known is the Unknown. The Unknown is God, some faint echo of whose Presence every great spiritual genius has given expression to. The Unknown Man is the *real* man. The known man is simply as much of a revelation of the Unknown as the intellect conceives at the present place in its evolution. The Universe is a spiritual system. Man is a part of this spiritual system. The spiritual system is perfect and the material universe is its counterpart. Therefore, the material universe, if we should rightly understand it, would be spiritual. This would not deny the reality of any objective form, but would include all form within Reality.

Those who have become aware of the spiritual Universe and who have come to understand the real nature of man, have taught us that the material universe is controlled by the spiritual; that the higher form of intelligence always governs the lower. From the standpoint of the spiritual Universe form or pattern determines the shape of substance. Substance conforms to the form. The findings of modern science tend to affirm this position.

The material universe is not a thing of itself, but it has a definite meaning. It is the expression of Spirit as substance according to the idea of form It has established. If we can accept this position as true, then come to understand that the nature of Spirit is to create and establish the pattern of the form, we can also understand how it is that man's intellect, as an aspect of infinite Intelligence, may be creative of the patterns which Spirit manifests as his experience.

In such degree as we understand this principle we shall be able to perform so-called miracles and it will all be in accord with Law. But we must first come to sense the spiritual Universe as real, and to know that the power of our word, as a mandate of Spirit within us, is immutable Law. To achieve this we have to learn to transpose the physical universe into terms of a spiritual one, and call upon the invisible side of ourselves. This is more than suggestion; it is the realization of the action of Life Itself. The Essence of Life is ever-present. But our intellectual and mental faculties create the mold this Essence takes in our experience. The Essence is already here; our conviction measures It out. We do not need to decry the intellect, but we do need to affirm that there is Spirit back of the intellect, using it but being greater than the thing It uses.

There is the intellectual man and there is the spiritual man, and the two comprise the experience of the human race. There is apparent cause and there is real Cause, but we must let that real Cause shine through. We must be sure that our realization of spiritual Reality is greater than our experience of the objective form. In other words, we must plunge beneath the objective form

13

to find the spiritual Cause. All spiritual mind treatment — prayer — is given, insofar as it is effective, from this spiritual viewpoint. It is plunging through the material and mental, and on the spiritual level remolding the pattern of the form. Prayer is effective only in such degree as we reach the conviction that we are dealing with that one Power which makes and remakes.

Therefore, we do not begin with the premise that man is basically material and subject to negation. As we view a negative objective fact we remind ourselves that it is like a picture projected upon a screen; then, turning from it as such, we get back to the mind that projects the picture and know that it is laboring under the illusion of false impressions. Our great illusion comes not from believing there is an objective world, but from believing that it is a thing of itself.

We yet know very little about the spiritual man — the man who can, by changing his mental images, reach out and transform his world of experience. We find ourselves in the forefront of the most advanced thought the world has ever known. The age in which we live is the first time in the entire history of the world when a definite and deliberate attempt is being made to teach everyone spiritual truths which may be specifically used.

Therefore, we see the opening of the transition of philosophy, of religion, and finally of science, from a material to a mental and spiritual concept of the Universe. There is gradually awakening in the human consciousness a concept of itself which is transcendent of the objective form. Every individual who lives can find that great *within* of himself which is immersed in God and is of God.

Man walks back and forth enslaved by the shadows of the walls he has erected between himself and Reality. The barriers are phantoms, misconceptions; they are not real. The Truth alone has the power to let the sunlight of the eternal God shine through the shadows of his imprisoned soul and set the captive free to know himself.

IDEAS TO LIVE BY

GOD-LIKE ARE SYMPATHY, COMPASSION, AND UNDER-
STANDING OF THE HUMAN, FOR THUS IS DIVINITY
UNVEILED.

ILLUMINED ARE THEY WHOSE LOVE INCLUDES BOTH
SAINT AND SINNER, FOR THEY SHALL KNOW LOVE.

BEAUTIFUL ARE ALL WHO THINK NO EVIL AND LISTEN
NOT TO FALSE REPORT OR UNKIND WORD. THEIR
FACES ARE GOOD TO LOOK UPON.

BLESSED ARE THEY TO WHOM GOODNESS ALONE IS
TRUE, FOR EVIL SHALL BE TO THEM AS THOUGH IT
WERE NOT.

IMMORTAL ARE ALL MEN. THE LIFE THEY LIVE TODAY
IS OF THE LIFE ETERNAL.

TRANQUIL ARE THEY WHOSE MINDS ARE AT PEACE.
THEY SHALL REFLECT A UNIVERSE OF POWER.

AFFLUENT ARE THEY WHO CONTEMPLATE SUBSTANCE,
FOR SUPPLY SHALL BE THEIRS.

INDEPENDENT ARE THEY WHO SHALL MIND THEIR
OWN AFFAIRS, FOR NO VIRTUE EXCELLETH THIS.

STRONG ARE THEY WHO CAN STAND IN AUTHORITY
WITHOUT ARROGANCE, FOR THEY SHALL STILL STAND.

2

THE POWER OF
YOUR MIND

*You and
the Universe*

The Universe is a spiritual system, an intelligent system; and we who live in It are surrounded by an infinite Presence which we call Spirit and an immutable Law which we call Mind in action, or the way Spirit works — cause and effect. We think of Spirit as infinite Intelligence acting as universal Law.

There must be an infinite Intelligence in the Universe which is conscious by reason of the fact that we are conscious. It would be impossible to describe the nature of this infinite Consciousness. We can only understand and realize It as we analyze our own natures which are akin to It. In other words, God is revealed by His presence or nature through what He does or creates.

The only thing we know anything about that has self-consciousness is man. Man is the highest development of the evolutionary process on this planet, hence must be the most nearly like his Source — the most Godlike. Man is an individual, or individualized being, and he could not be an individualized being unless that from which he comes, the Source of his being, is in a universal sense the infinite Essence of all being. Therefore, we have every logical reason to suppose that there is an infinite Presence or Person in the universe. The Whole must contain in Itself the essence of all Its parts.

We wish to, and we must, arrive at what we consider to be a correct conclusion independent of other people's opinions and theological speculations. Otherwise we may become mesmerized by our own confused thoughts. We may survey what anyone has taught if we so desire, but for ourselves we must be the judge and the jury as to our final conclusions; there is no other judge or jury. We cannot arrive at truth unless we arrive at it independent of the hypnotic influence of those we believe to have known a lot more about things than we do. Many widespread traditions have been built up through the blind acceptance of false concepts, and more and more people have come to believe them until there has been such an unquestioning acceptance of them that they are now acknowledged as true and unchallengeable.

We must arrive at conclusions by common sense, by a fearless ability to look at the manifestation of things and examine and weigh them and take their full measurement. Then finally accept not what someone else taught but what we find reason to conclude for ourselves. We are to become the interpreters of the Universe rather than accepting others as the only interpreters and their findings the only final truths. Each of us, through our inner nature, has direct access to our Source; we need no intermediary but ourselves.

Wherever scientific men have looked they have seen law in action, therefore they often have concluded that the material universe is completely a mechanistic system, a huge engine. But now we find scientists beginning to discuss the possibility of an Engineer. The idea that everything was predetermined mechanistically is rapidly disappearing from science and the era upon which we are entering is discovering volition and purpose in the universe. Science is now giving God back to religion — a greater God than previously conceived of — and itself is again coupling the engine with the Engineer. All this will probably help to create a new and more all-encompassing religious viewpoint which will be both scientific and spiritual; it will deal with the Law which is orderly and just, and at the same time it will deal with the Divine Presence which is warm and colorful.

We are to seek to draw inspiration from the Divine Presence, and then use the Divine Law for specific purposes. We are to

consciously combine what is called the personal and the impersonal elements of the Universe into the one Unity which they
already are. This is what great modern thinkers, with a com-
prehension of things as they really are, are trying to do.

However, even in the field of modern thought ideas concern-
ing these two factors differ. There are those who look upon the
infinite Presence merely as an infinite Principle and such persons
overlook the necessity of warmth and color and become psychologically cold. Such people do not smile spontaneously; there
is always a degree of inflexibility in their thinking and a rigidity
in their emotions. We do not desire that. While we are to realize
that everything is Law, we are also to realize that Law is a servant;
It is something to be used by the warm, impulsing Presence. We
must avoid any prejudice or lack of knowledge which will reduce
us either to the position of the extreme sentimentalists or to the
position of the extreme materialists.

We need a balance and as we study the nature of the manifest
universe we shall find that it is perfectly balanced. Without
compensation there would be no balance. Without cause and
effect we would have an Intelligence with no expression, and
a Mind that does not express anything is a nonentity. The first
law of consciousness is that it must be conscious of something.
In other words, there must always be the Thing, the way It
works, and how to use It. We are to combine the idea of the engine — a universe of law and order — with the Engineer — an
absolute Intelligence which is conscious of Itself, setting in mo-
tion creative forces that produce the logical result of a Self-contemplation of Itself. We ourselves, by very reason of the fact
that we exist, are some part of this system, and there is *something*
which receives the impress of our thought and acts upon it.

Our evolution is not a creation or the result of a creation of
Intelligence cast into a void, but is the result of the unfolding
of Intelligence in and through us as what we are. Instead of saying that our intelligence is the result of evolution, we say evolution is the result of Intelligence. And is it not true that everything

18

to which we awaken, everything of which the human race has ever become aware, existed before there was awareness of it? Our evolution is an awakening to what was before we awoke to it, because our awakening to it could not produce that which was not. We awaken to existing principles which we may use uniquely and in so doing produce a new thing. But the new thing is made out of that which always has been, and by a method which was always possible. This demonstrates not a new possibility, but a new form resulting from a new awareness.

The creative Principle is forever pushing forward into new things, and It is personified in us. It often seems as though we were limiting the Divine idea, but we are not. We are expressions of God, however we ourselves are but gods "though in the germ." We do not yet fully understand our own natures. We seem to relegate to the realm of the unnatural those things which we alone shall discover to be real.

We are to uncover the Spirit, finding that it is the Spirit which dominates the letter of the Law. The Spirit is the spontaneous Presence, the Law is simply the way It works. As we look about us we see that everything conforms to law and order; our world in its functioning is mechanical; it is a stupendous engine. But when we add the Engineer we have a perfect Whole. We should accept the physical universe as it is, knowing that its mechanical operation according to law and order is necessary. However, we should seek to combine the warm, colorful Presence with the immutable Law, then the Engineer will be running the engine!

Out of this balancing and blending of Spirit and Law we may evolve a system of thought which we can definitely use in shaping and reshaping our experiences so that we are free of stress. These are the tools with which we work in creating a new life.

3

YOUR INNER
RESOURCES

*All Creation
Is for You*

We spring up out of the Universe — countless individuals, innumerable people, all having the same Source yet all different. If we all looked exactly alike and acted exactly alike, what monotony could be more infinite? Everything tends to prove that the Universe is pouring Itself out into innumerable individual forms, but we are rooted in one Substance. We know of the eternality of Energy, of the eternality of the Stuff which becomes form, of the eternality of Mind which creates the pattern of the form. Out of God, or Spirit, which is Life, form and substance merge through what we call evolution. We are part of It, and we are the part of It that is able to reflect upon the rest of It. We are self-conscious individuals. God could not project as individuality unless the Divine Mind and universal Principle projecting it pushed Itself into that individuality and became it, thereby remaining in a unique and infinite sense personal to that which It individualizes as.

Any man who persists in believing that the Universe is personal to that which is individualized will never be wrong. Any man is wrong who denies that *that* which individualizes lacks some universal type of personalness. In other words, he would be in the impossible position of saying that we have gotten out of the bag something which is not in it.

From the scientific viewpoint we find that there is not only a science, there is also a scientist. There is not only a thought, there is a thinker. There is not only an accomplishment, there is a will. There is back of every man that which is God. There is, from this Source, an individualized flow, a personified point — personality and humanity are Divine. We are immersed in the One Mind, One Intelligence; we are indivisible from It.

"He that planted the ear, shall he not hear? . . . he that formed the eye, shall he not see? . . . he that teacheth man knowledge, shall not he know?" To put it in other words: Is it intelligent to believe that the Spirit which projects as individuality is impersonal to that which It becomes? Of course not! But we must think of It not as a limiting, but as a limitless Source, which means that within every man there is a wise Counsellor.

This raises the question: Does God consciously impart to us? Can we listen to the Divine and learn how to invent a machine, how to write a play or a song? It happens that we can. But does God specialize on some people? There is no such thing as a special dispensation of providence. God does not like Mary better than he does Martha, or John better than he does Bill or Jim. God likes us all alike. But when some of us like God better than others, then it looks as though God were giving us special attention because we specialize, but we only present a better inlet and outlet. We look at men like Edison or Burbank and see what marvels they revealed. And then people say that these men are uniquely blessed, God is doing everything for them. They are right — God is. Why? Because they listened!

Emerson said that we should learn to listen greatly to ourself and watch that spark of genius that flashes across our thought. He said that the greatness we ascribe to Jesus and Moses and Plato is the result of the fact that they listened to what they themselves thought and not to what other men said. This is a great and wonderful and daring thing to do. Many people, doing it, listen only to their desires, and their desires personify and they believe that God has spoken and told them what to say. These people are having hallucinations. And yet God speaks to the listening ear, and if the ear that listens is intelligent, what happens is sane.

God speaks when we listen. God is there when we open the door. And when we listen there is a response from *something* greater than we are which is the infinite Person, the limitless Possibility. God speaks wherever we let Him, and the man who receives the most has become most God-like in his nature.

To make this practical we must listen, but we must listen deliberately, with definite intention, so that the Spirit may speak to us. We shall have to be certain that we are not merely answering our own desires with thought forms and pictures from our subjective nature. Our acts will demonstrate whether or not the message we receive is correct. If a man says he has an inspiration from God and then does something that contradicts every rule of reason, we will know that his inspiration is not from God. Nothing that comes from God will ever be chaotic.

We need a God with whom we can communicate. We need more than a Principle. To be sure, we want a Principle; we must have a Principle, for when we give a spiritual mind treatment we want to know that it embodies the Power of Divine Principle, and that it will work. But we cannot feel the law that two and two make four; we can know it. We cannot feel the facts of science, but we can sense the scientist. So, to science we must add feeling, without which it is dead. The letter of the Law without the Spirit is bereft because the Spirit is superior to and the user of the Law.

Beyond our metaphysical abstractions, beyond the mere use of the Principle, there must come a dawning consciousness of the Presence. There is a Presence in the universe, and if we would see back of the performance to It, then we should add color, joy, beauty, and harmony to the performance. This would mean that each one of us has a Divine and infinite Companion. It is the Spirit of which we are the direct individualizations. It is personal to us. It is more intelligent than our intellects, and the demand that our intellects make upon It is answered by Its own Self-pronouncement.

22

Back of each of us is both the Principle and the Presence, a Divine Unity. What should we do with It? We should cultivate It. It comes to us only as the expression of our true self. God and man are not separated, and any separation that seems to exist is only in our belief. Consequently, the whole mind should be open to that Divine influx to which each is a center, and each being a center may become a source of all the information that is potential.

Whenever we create an idea it is because a demand has been made upon the Mind which is incarnated in us. The Mind which is in us at once answers the demand in terms of Its own embodiment, and reveals as much of Itself as our intellects are equipped to receive. It is beating against us now, It is in us now, It is around us now, but we mentally measure out what we shall receive in terms of the limitations of our previous experiences. But little by little we can grow, and experience adds to experience and we accumulate an ever greater possibility.

Each one is a direct inlet and direct outlet to God. Why should we not add to our concept of Law the knowledge of this infinite Personalness residing within us? It is never limited by or separated from us except by the degree of our own ignorance. It is the same to all, but to each unique and entirely different, and is always instantly available to rightly guide and direct us through the vicissitudes of living.

4

LEARN TO LIVE ABUNDANTLY

Create a
Better Tomorrow

It seems that man exists for the purpose of self-expression. There appears to be no other reason or excuse for his being. The Infinite has already implanted within man an instinctive intuition which is the spiritual knowledge of good, and his whole growth results from an inner awakening.

Just as fast as man understands a law, that law is his servant, for he then consciously uses a power which until he used it remained dormant so far as he was concerned. Man has discovered many laws and every newly discovered law tends to give him greater freedom. He is now awaking to the Law of Mind which will give him still greater freedom, but he is discovering that as his thought reaches out into the higher Law, It is not delivered to him for Its full and complete usage, in Its full constructiveness, until he himself imbibes the spirit of this Law, which is the spirit of truth, of unity, of harmony, of love, of reason, of beauty, and of a common unitary life.

This does not mean that nature refuses to reveal physical laws to man for destructive purposes, because that is not so. Man studies physics and chemistry, he learns how to make high explosives, and even harness the basic power of nature with which he may destroy himself. He has that much freedom. Nature does enable man to use its laws even for destructive purposes, there is no doubt about that. The same wind that will blow a boat safely into the harbor can also wreck it; electricity will

24

warm a man's feet and cook his dinner, but it also will electrocute him. However, we find as we come into a knowledge of the fundamental creative Law of Life that It will not surrender Itself to a use other than good.

Every great thinker has proclaimed this. Jesus announced it when they accused him of casting out devils by Beelzebub, the Prince of Devils, and he said that that is not possible, for that would be a house divided against itself. And he added that he did this with the knowledge of God. Emerson, who is considered by some as one of the greatest thinkers who has ever lived, said: "Nature forevermore screens herself from the profane. . . . If a man will subject himself to this doctrine he will understand the will from whence it comes." This is exactly what Jesus meant when he said: " . . . seek ye first the kingdom of God [the kingdom of Unity, of Righteousness, of Good, of Truth] . . . and all these things shall be added unto you."

That brings out and emphasizes the idea that supply is a spiritual concept. At once someone will say, "That may be so, but I know a man who is a miserable sinner yet he has plenty of money." Don't we all? Also we know men who are miserable sinners and have no money. Who knows any man who is not a miserable sinner, ourselves included? But God does not judge people that way. God is that eternal Presence which forever delivers Itself in the terms of Its own being. Many people are being born into the world every day who bring nothing with them, apparently; and who has ever attended a funeral and seen the departed take anything with him? So it appears that there is no external wealth which amounts to anything if it can be lost or left behind. And yet the kind of wealth that is eternal must at the same time provide the kind of wealth that is temporal according to the Law of Good.

That is what Jesus taught about substance and supply. He did not say that it is wicked to have money, that it is wrong to have your bread buttered on both sides if you like it that way. He did say that everyone is rewarded according to the way he uses Life —

"Verily I say unto you, They have their reward." But he added that if you want a wealth that will give you whatever you need in this life, and at the same time cause you to know that you shall have everything you need in the next life, that wealth is contained in a consciousness of the kingdom of God — seek that first and secondary things will be added.

In other words, Jesus taught that that which is worthwhile in this life is merely added to that which always will be worthwhile here and in the next life. There would be no sense in anything without a belief in immortality. So, believing in it, we find that there must be a Law which is not only operative in this life, but in the next. In a going to sleep to this life and awaking to the next one the great Law of Life will not change during our transition. Wherever we go from here we are going to have a continuation of whatever we have become while on this physical plane. We need to recognize that Law which will free us here, and also heal us of the fear of the hereafter.

We want to have abundance while we are here, and there seems to be nothing wrong with that. Perhaps some think that is a materialistic doctrine, but if life exists for self-expression, why it is wrong to express the self? Moreover, even those who deny it is right want it just the same! Substance is God, Substance is Spirit, supply is a manifestation of this invisible Substance; therefore, there is a spiritual idea back of it. If we wish to demonstrate happiness, success, and abundance in whatever we do in this life, then it is certain that if there is a Law which cannot deny it, in such degree as we imbibe the spirit of that Law right action cannot be denied us. Just as the light will overcome the darkness, so a knowledge of limitless supply will destroy poverty. But the question might be asked: "There is so much poverty in the world; what finally will destroy all poverty?" Only this: when the majority of people think straight, and understand that good is not individual, but universal. When fear is removed from the human mind, poverty will be eliminated in the human family. Nature has already provided an abundance.

Now we, individually, probably will not live in this world long enough to see fear eliminated from man's thinking. We can have no such expectation. So the question is: Are we going to be able to eliminate fear in our own individual minds? If so, then we shall be adding that much to the elimination of fear in the race mind and by that degree hasten the recognition of the expression of the Divine through the human, which will provide everything that we need. The problem, to begin with, is individual, for social systems are the result of collective individual convictions. The elimination of poverty, disease, and unhappiness from the face of the earth can only begin with the individual, where he now is, and he will succeed to the extent he permits the Divine Abundance to flow into his life.

Jesus had such a consciousness of supply that he could multiply loaves and fishes. We do not know how he did it, but it is not hard for us to believe it was done. Some may say that is contradictory to every known law. But newly discovered and revolutionary laws often supersede older known laws. The Universe is filled with transcendent laws which are just as real as the ones we call ordinary laws; but the ordinary laws are ordinary to us merely because we understand them. Therefore, it does not seem strange that a man with the understanding of Jesus could hasten the process of creativity and instantly provide a manifestation of Substance which nature already provides through a slower process. Jesus had such a sufficient consciousness of the Spirit that the time involved in the process was eliminated, having no cognizance of itself.

If, then, we had a consciousness of limitless Substance today should we not discover our supply today? We might achieve this consciousness over a period of time by a process of evolution and growth and unfoldment; that is generally the way it comes and maybe it is better that it comes that way. However, to deny the possibility of the instantaneous manifestation of the Absolute in the relative is to deny the Absolute, and we would not wish to do that. Therefore, we find that the process of time in demonstration is eliminated in such degree as there is a consciousness of instantaneous fulfillment. If it takes six months to get the answer in one's own mind, it is good when one gets it. But suppose one could get it today! Today the answer would have to exist because the answer has never departed from the Universe; it has always been in God, in the Mind of God, so to speak.

And so we come to the conclusion that in demonstrating supply as a spiritual idea we must not procrastinate our day of good to some theoretical tomorrow. Perhaps that is what the poet intuitively had in mind: " . . . for to-morrow and its needs, / I do not pray; / But keep me, guide me, love me, Lord, / Just for to-day." And that is what Jesus meant when he said: " . . . when ye pray, believe that ye receive. . . . " This is the secret of effective prayer, and it is according to a Law which is easy to understand.

When we pray or give a spiritual mind treatment it is something we do to our own mind to convert it to a new belief. It is a change from a belief in evil to a belief in good, from a belief in lack to a belief in abundance, from fear to faith. We convince our mind that our good, the abundance we desire, is now here. But so much of our life is a meditation on lack, isn't it? When we talk with others we talk about lack; when we read, we read about it. We are afraid of it, and the thing which we fear, by reason of a neutral Law, brings the feared thing upon us.

Someone might ask: "But does this apply if I want an automobile, a house, a dress?" Yes, why not? There is nothing of more importance than something else to the Power that creates and supplies all; there is no big and no little to It. The painting of a picture that expresses life and beauty is just as important in the Divine scheme of things as the creation of a cosmos. It takes every man's wholeness to produce the great mosaic of life.

It is right that we should be happy. What good is suffering and misery? It is all wrong; it does no one any good; it does not please God; it does not help man's evolution. But if that is the only way we can learn, then we will have to learn that way.

Either by pure spiritual intuition or perception, or by bitter experience, humanity is brought at last to the realization of Good. We can short-circuit the hardships of negative experiences if we have enough spiritual vision to do it. Even the trivial things of life, if they express life, are good. People do not have enough fun, they do not seem to have enough of anything. And unfortunately, those who appear to have a lot of things are so afraid of losing them that they do not enjoy them. Riches are not good if one is afraid to use them, or if they pile up so that they become cumbersome. The only thing that is any good in life is the thing that is being used. The Divine intends us to have abundance, but abundance must be accepted and used.

It is not selfish for us to desire to succeed, to express life, to have everything that makes us happy. But it would be selfish if we desired such at someone else's expense. If we take that which we will not give, by the same Law someone can take from us that which we cannot appear to get back. That is the only robbery there is. In the long run there is no law but our own soul shall set it, under the great Divine Law of Life. If we have no desire to hurt, if we believe absolutely in good, if we accept that a spiritual idea can cause the Infinite to manifest in our experience as supply, then we will find coming into our immediate environment everything that makes life worthwhile.

Our prayer, spiritual mind treatment, should be both general and specific. It is not enough to say that God is good. Unconsciously we believe it, but we should liken that goodness with ours. Suppose we sent a company of electrical engineers up into the high mountains and when they returned they reported having discovered a great waterfall that no one knew existed, the energy of which would light and heat every building and run all the machinery in the state. We would say, "Isn't that marvelous!" Suppose the next year we sent someone to the same place and he returned and said, "Yes, it is there." Then suppose we all got together and exclaimed, "O wonderful energy in the high mountains, enough to light and heat every building and run all the machinery in the state! O marvelous, wonderful energy!" But there would not be a light lighted or a house warmed or a wheel turned. What does that teach us? That the forces of nature are of value only to the extent that man desires to make use of such forces.

This is true of the Law of Mind. Because all laws are spiritual, as we discover and study the laws of nature we also shall be discovering the Law of Mind. All the forces of nature operate according to real, definite laws, and only because of this can the energy of the waterfall be utilized. And when it comes to the great Energy of Divine Mind it is the same thing. Of course It is there — a Divine Mind which knows everything, and is the potential of all knowledge. We are surrounded by an Intelligence that knows exactly what we ought to do, and how to do it. But we do not know all that It knows, and It can only know for us what we know It knows.

Suppose we have a problem to solve. Just as the waterfall in the mountains must be discovered before its potential power may be usefully directed into our lives, so there must be a general recognition of the Divine Potential followed by a specialized application of It to our problem. That is the technique involved in giving a spiritual mind treatment.

Spirit creates for us in our experience according to the pattern of thought which we give It. Spirit is universal, limitless potential, and ever ready to express. We may specialize It. Therefore, if, for instance, we are treating a condition of disagreement among some people, we say, "God is all there is, there is only One Mind." That is true before we say it. But we add (and we are not trying to control or hypnotize these people): "There is One Mind, that is the Mind of these people. No misunderstanding has ever arisen in that Mind, no fear, no hate, no separation; that which appears to be separated is really united, and as a result of Law acting through my word all disagreement is forgiven, forgotten, and wiped out."

That is bringing the unity of the Mind of God to bear upon

a certain problem, just as we direct the power of the waterfall to light a room. We must first recognize the broad general principle underlying everything — God is all there is. Then we consider the specific problem in view of this larger concept and sense that this infinite Power is the solution of this problem; that It now projects Itself into our experience in a certain definite manner to resolve the whole problem. But suppose we do not know how to act or what to do? How are we going to be specific? This always can be done by knowing that although we do not now appear to have such conscious knowledge, there is an Intelligence around us and in us that will supply it to us. We then may receive the consciousness of the needed idea and it is received with the Power that enables it to project itself into form.

We are subject to and the servant of the thing we believe in, always. Man makes his own laws and then falls down and worships them and believes they are immutable. But a true knowledge of God looses the potentiality of all Being, and we may use it.

If we are to consider money as a spiritual idea, then we must know that God is Substance and Substance is supply; that Substance is now, today, manifesting Itself as supply in our experience. Therefore, we translate the idea of money into its equivalent, supply. Then we must see our supply as emanating from the infinite Source which is forever surrounding us, flowing into and reflecting through everything we do. As the Divine gives us ideas, we act upon them, and gradually we find things beginning to improve in our environment. The process is long or short according to our state of consciousness. So we should spend our time re-creating our own concept of good: "God is Substance, God is my supply. His Substance now, through definite Law, is the supply of my experience. Every good thing comes to me, and only good goes out from me."

Suppose we do that and it does not work. Just remember this: "Act as though I am, and I will be." That is one of the wisest things ever said. If we try and fail there is nothing to do but to try again, and perhaps try in a better way. Perhaps we need to be a little more certain that we are not limiting the Divine Principle to what we consider as unchangeable facts. God makes facts just as fast as God images, pictures, or contemplates His own Being. So out of our contemplation, out of our prayer or treatment, shall be established a new fact which shall correspond and be equivalent to the form of that idea envisioned in the treatment. Indwelling every soul there *is* a Divine Something, call It what you will, that is creative of our destiny.

5

YOUR MENTAL DIET

The Key to
Health

It might have sounded very strange to speak of a mental diet a number of years ago, but it does not seem at all strange today. The idea of physical diet, which has largely been a fad, is gradually being reduced to a science. We all know that certain foods affect us in definite ways. But any physician will tell us that diet is largely an individual thing and that, generally speaking, one should eat what he likes, be glad to eat it, and not worry while he is eating it.

The newest contributions to the subject of diet are those of biochemistry, the chemistry of the human body. It is very interesting that we find that many physical troubles are the result of glandular deficiences and psychological upsets. There is no doubt that back of many glandular deficiencies there is a mental or emotional imbalance, which, of course, is what the psychiatrists tell us. They do not deny the physical deficiency; they merely affirm that in many cases it arises out of a mental disturbance.

David Seabury once wrote about "psychic pus," as one would speak of any infection in the physical body. But this means a subjective, a subconscious, and primarily a mental state. So while the physician and the biochemist are telling us what is good to eat to compensate for our chemical deficiencies, we should go a step farther and cooperate with them by providing a mental diet, for without a proper mental attitude a physical diet is seldom complete enough to do anything other than produce a temporary cure.

Mental causation is invisible and largely emotional. We also find that spiritual inspiration and spiritual realization are necessary to a well-regulated mental life. The physician diagnoses the body and prescribes a remedy; so does the phychiatrist. Both are good, each is necessary; however, many leading authorities have said that unless the mind is more spiritually oriented there cannot be a permanent healing. There is a growing tendency in the field of psychiatry to return the patient to some aspect of religion. This is an amazing confession that the individual does not live by bread alone.

What thoughts and emotional states, then, are back of certain types of disease? This is a sphere of activity of interest to us. The actual treatment of the physical body is the province of medical men. We are interested in getting at the possible mental cause of the physical disorder for until we do that the medical help provided could easily be of little value. In many cases of pernicious anemia an emotional imbalance has been discovered. Just as biochemistry may tell us about a chemical deficiency, we may speak of an emotional deficiency — a lack of a sense of being appreciated and loved. There can be no permanent healing, as Jung says, without a restoration of faith; and in this case the faith must be of the same intensity as the lack which produced the deficiency. There must come a specific faith in *love,* a consciousness that within the infinite Love of God is included all finite love. The awareness of this will again produce affection, cooperation, human companionship and affiliation in the life of the individual. He will have reorganized his thinking and emotions. The mental deficiency, which was primarily an emotional one, will be changed.

It is a common belief that many heart conditions are the result of extreme tension. What is the mental deficiency here? It appears to be a lack of that kind of faith which knows that everything is going to be all right. The tension will be released and the person will be helped, in every instance, if he is freed of a sense of stress and strain. But what thought could accomplish this desired result other than the thought that "underneath are the everlasting arms"? As Browning said, "It is thou, God, who givest; it is I who receive."

Many who suffer from gastrointestinal troubles can be helped if they are released from thoughts of irritation, agitation, and inflammation. There needs to be established a spiritual equivalent, a prototype of peace, of a sense of completion — no overaction or wrong action in the mind of the individual.

It seems that the majority of people who have trouble with their throats, if they could get over having their feelings hurt would be helped and probably most of them healed. We also find that stomach ulcers are seldom developed by phlegmatic, unemotional people; nor do we often find phelgmatic, callous, or hard-boiled people having nervous prostration. Many physical ailments are the result of a mind that turns upon itself. Why do people's minds turn morbidly within? Because they are not adjusted to the world in which they live.

Remember Coue's axiom that when the imagination and will are in conflict, the imagination always wins. The imagination and feeling are creative where the will is only directive. So the will, the imagination, and the feeling must come into conjunction, into mutual agreement, before there is a right mental life. And the only thing that has ever brought them into mutual agreement is a recognition of that *something* man considers bigger than himself — a belief in the spiritual Universe. It is just as impossible to divorce spiritual values from a well-ordered mental world as it is to take the heat out of fire. The body is not an entity in itself, nor is the mind; neither could be changed if they were, therefore we must believe in a supreme Power — God.

It must be that back of a physical disturbance there is some mental cause. If we examine the nature of the physical condition we will at least be able to partly diagnose the mental cause and anyone who can ascertain the mental cause can prescribe a mental remedy which will at least be helpful. Such a mental remedy would necessarily be a thought and emotional reaction that is not only directly opposite to the one that produced the sick body, but one which possesses a complete conviction to the contrary. We are dealing with Law and we cannot fool It, therefore the conviction must be both deep and sincere. For all the words we may use are meaningless unless there is unquestioning belief in them. The power of Jesus to heal was not in the particular words he used, but in that consciousness back of those words which had the knowledge of the full significance and meaning of them

Hence the one who would prescribe for himself a mental diet for health must drink deeply at the spiritual fountain of his own life; he must catch the fire of heaven in his own imagination. It is only through the awareness and acceptance of the nature and power of that *something* greater than he is that he may come to experience Its peace and perfection in his own life.

PART TWO

NEW APPROACHES TO LIVING

No problem, difficulty, or negative situation in living was ever corrected by doing nothing about it. Neither can it be brought under control by thinking only the worst about it. In fact, nothing worthwhile has ever been accomplished through a defeatist attitude. Achievement is the result of knowing that a thing is possible, followed by action commensurate with the knowing. A positive and affirmative approach is the only way to confront those stress-creating factors which continually impinge on you.

Through your thought you have the ability to draw on your inner resources wherein lie the power and the direction to enable you to surmount undesirable situations and conditions in your experience.

The nature of the life you are living first begins with an idea. The ideas you continually maintain are the determinants. If you are to find a new life, a new freedom from your damaging reactions, it becomes obligatory to create a new and affirmative outlook. Your experiences are but the reflections of the contents of your own mind.

6

FREEDOM FROM LIMITATION

*What You Want,
You Have!*

The world in which we live is basically spiritual and mental, and has its source in one ultimate Reality. It is the nature of this Reality to desire and to seek expression, and it is Its nature to realize and fulfill Its desire through Its own immutable Law. The physical laws exist as the ways and the means through which It works in creating effects. But effects have an intelligent Causation back of them, an immutable Law governing them, and there is an individualization of the Infinite permeating them. And man, of necessity, is part of the Wholeness which encompasses everything. Very simple, isn't it?

However, if we would stick to these few fundamental propositions, we should understand all the wisdom the ages have given us. It is because we have so covered up that wisdom with inconsistency that we see only a little of it through the small crack we in our ignorance forget to cover. We must insist that the Truth is simple and direct. If we are to understand the spiritual philosophies and pronouncements of the ages we must believe and understand that God creates out of Himself, by Himself directly becoming the thing that He makes, and, as Jesus said, what God does we can do!

With this in mind we see that we do have untapped Power at the center of our being. We already have what we seek. We already possess what we are trying to acquire. Heaven is lost merely for the lack of the idea of harmony, and hell is merely a state of consciousness peopled with the phantoms of our own morbid imagery. In other words, to use a very colloquial expression, the Universe eternally "passes the buck" straight back to the individual and says: "Take it or leave it, there it is." Referring to the nature of the Divine Being, the Old Testament twice states, in Samuel and in Psalms: "With the pure thou wilt shew thyself pure; and with the froward thou wilt shew thyself froward." We know that is true. Life is to each one of us what we are to It.

We have Power, but we must use It. We find among our chief difficulties: first, we do not believe that we have It; next, we do not understand that we can use It. Now why? Let us analyze these two great negations. They are environmental and traditional; they have been with us so many ages that they have now become what may be called instinctive. Many of the things which we call instinctive have been acquired by a habit of thought that has gone on so long we cannot even figure it out. Always people have been afraid of God. Only once in a while we find individuals who have not been afraid of God — people like Jesus, Buddha, Emerson, Whitman, and others. They understood that there was nothing to be afraid of but themselves.

There is the traditional idea that we could not be good enough to have a Divine Power within us, while, as a matter of fact, we could not be bad enough to get rid of It. Whether we acknowledge it or not, we are neither so good nor so bad that we can avoid being a product of the Universe. This belief that we are not good enough to use Divine Power arises out of superstition as well as a vulgar interpretation of the Universe through a false theology.

The belief that we have the Power but we do not know how to use It — which belief we find very widespread — is just as invalid. We seem to think we have to wait and wait and wait. If someone should say to us, "You don't know how to use It," let us respond that we do not know how to stop using It. We are using this Power every time we think. What we ought to do, then, is to use It consciously instead of unconsciously. Too largely our previous use of It is now using us and we are captives of our misuse of freedom. We have a creative consciousness, but by a previous misdirected use of it we have availed ourselves of the action of the Law which now tends to limit us.

We have this creative Power but we are afraid of It because we are afraid of the idea of God. Our thoughts of God have always been rather terrifying, but now that we admit that we are expressions of the Divine and there is a Creativeness in us, we still say, "Well, we do not have enough understanding to use It." We need somebody to shake us into a sensibility that we *are using* Divine Creativity — It is always working for us! Consequently, what we need is a constructive and conscious use, but what does that imply? It implies sometimes a spiritual contradiction of a material sense of things. Jesus put it another way when he said: "Judge not according to the appearance, but judge righteous judgment." For instance, the sun does not rise and set; it looks as though it does. When everybody believed that the world was flat, the world was still round; the belief did not flatten the world, but it flattened the experience of people. In other words, nothing that you and I can think can destroy God, but what we think about God can limit our experience of God to the confines of our thought.

We have to realize that the Truth is that which does not permit of limitation, but which does appear to permit of what we call a limited use of It. Is the principle of mathematics limited because we can only count up to seven? No. How many people can count up to seven, or use the figures one, two, and so forth, without wearing them out? Did we ever stop to think that everybody in the world could use all the number sevens he wanted to and there would be just as many number sevens left as when he started? That is what it means to be dealing with an infinite Universe. The infinite and limitless Universe delivers Itself to us in terms of our use of It. We may measure It out and limit our experience of It, but not It. Such a freedom is actually our guarantee of our experience, and if we are going to use this Power inherent in us, consciously and constructively, let us realize again that it is the nature of desire to fulfill itself.

It appears that the whole evolutionary process in man has been a continual development in him of possibilities which he has gradually learned to fully use. Today man's use of his legs and hands is far advanced from that time in the dim past when he first began to experiment with them. Similarly, there has been the continual development of mind and self-consciousness in man. Now man finds himself endowed with a mind with which he can consciously conceive and create, but his fuller use of this ability must await his greater awareness and acceptance of it. Life has brought man thus far, but beyond this he must learn to use what has been given him.

Jesus said something which refers to this: " . . . My Father worketh hitherto, and I work." This is a mystical saying, full of spiritual import and tremendous meaning. To us it can mean that through the process of evolution the creative Principle of the Universe developed man by arbitrary methods; there was a compulsion behind his development. Then the arbitrary processes of evolution seem to have stopped and waited, because now there had developed a free-thinking center resembling its Source. Further evolvement implies that there must be cooperation between man and God. The Mind of God is now extended and individualized in man, who is backed by the Power of God and so nicely adjusted to the eternal Harmony that when he seeks to do wrong he hurts and punishes himself, and when he finally learns to do right he discovers that he is rewarded.

We may be absolutely certain that whenever and wherever our desire is constructive no harm can ever come from it to ourselves or anyone else, and any idea of good can never fail to demonstrate itself. We need not be afraid of the Universe. It is going to be all right; It is foolproof. It is we who appear to be foolish, yet there is a Wisdom in us that senses and perceives Its own reality.

Our experiences are the direct results of our own states of mind, and nothing else. What is more simple or more just than that we, ourselves, should be the final arbiters of our own fates? Why should not a good man enjoy peace of mind? Why should not an intelligent man be happy? Why should not a man who tries to sense the kingdom of God as now present be provided with everything he wants at this particular point on the road of the kingdom of God? Our trouble is that we still think we are living in a material universe and are waiting to shuffle off this plane into a spiritual Universe. We fail to realize that we are living in a spiritual Universe *now*. All that is is an expression of the Divine. The Spirit manifests Itself in and as tangible form, the physical universe as well as ourselves. The Essence and Source of everything resolves into that which is not seen — spiritual Reality. Fundamentally we can never possess more of a spiritual nature than we now have, but we can become more aware of it.

It seems that our intellectual difficulty is that we do not see the subtlety of this thing. It is simple enough to understand, but it is not easy to practice because we like to indulge in our extravagant reactions to life. We like to get mad, we like to damn everybody who does not believe as we believe. But poverty is not a virtue, sickness is not a sign of spiritual growth. If we were to analyze and diagnose all our petty virtues and petty vices, I am not sure which would come out ahead, or which would be the worst.

So, if we want to use this Thing consciously and definitely we must no longer deny that It exists. It is simple but it is not easy to think success in the midst of failure, for instance. It is not easy in the midst of pain to think of peace. It is not easy when everyone says we are fools to believe in ourselves. We have to contradict much. Do we really believe that God is all there is? Yes, theoretically we believe it, but now we must begin to practice that belief. In actual practice we must see what we want instead of what we do not want. Someone will say, "You may see what you want but don't you realize you are up against it? Don't you realize that every door is closed?" All right, let them be closed, another is being opened right in front of us! We must come to believe in the absoluteness of our spiritual nature. There is *Something* within us that sees no obstruction and walks right through it, by some Law of Its own.

It is the nature of desire to seek self-expression; it is the nature of God to be fulfilled; it is the nature of man to be like God. We want love, friendship, happiness, health. These are spiritual qualities. There is no reason why we should not desire them. Certainly the right use of beauty is harmony; certainly the right use of law is order; certainly the right understanding of truth is freedom. These must be immediately perceived in our own thought. Each must say to himself, and come to believe, that he is surrounded by love, by friendship, by Divine guidance.

It is most important that we shall interpret the abstract essence of Spirit as being manifested in terms of our needs as they arise in our human experience. If a man needs a dollar or a loaf of bread he must interpret the Divine as fulfilling that need. If we can become so accustomed to the knowledge that the Law of Good will provide us with all our needs, we shall be provided. What a marvelous thing it would be to come to know that at all times we shall meet love, and experience prosperity, happiness, success — every good we desire.

7

START TO REALLY LIVE

Existence Is
Not Enough

Life is something we cannot avoid. Life is, and we can do nothing about it other than accept it and use it and live it, for it will always be that way. We have always existed as a potential person in the Mind of God and now that that potential person is projected, he can never cease to be. We did not create our own soul; it is some part of God. We can no more be extinguished than God can be extinguished. But that is not the problem which confronts us.

The problem is this: We live, but how? That is the only problem there is. Because we are individuals we may be happy or unhappy; we may be certain or uncertain; we may be morbid and afraid, or we may live now as though we were already in the kingdom of heaven. And so Life presents Itself to us after the images of our reactions to It.

All of our experiences may be true; even that may be true which lasts only temporarily. Even mistakes are true as experiences. We might write on the blackboard: Two plus two equals thirteen. Now, of course, the Reality is that two plus two equals four, but it is a true fact that it was written that two plus two equals thirteen. Our experience of what is true is always changing because it is the best we know at any particular time. So we have to distinguish between objective truth and ultimate Reality, which remains changeless.

Psychology has proved that it is not the unhappy experience

we have that hurts us; it is our emotional reaction to the experience. The imprint of the experience made upon the mind is indelible, but it is only our continued reactions to that imprint that may cause us to remain morbid or unhappy. It has been stated that one of the most difficult things the analytical psychologist has to do is to redirect such an emotional response because there is an inertia in a mental habit which at times acts as though it were a person, and, as it were, seeks to argue that it shall not be disturbed.

It is not the experience we have, then, but it is the emotional reaction to it which plays havoc with us. If we can catch the emotional reaction quickly enough and put it where it belongs by saying, "I have decided not to let this thing destroy my happiness," we shall be doing well. If we lose a friend, we are sorry that we have lost that friend because we loved him, and that is only natural. We do not want to so harden our thought that nothing affects us; there is a warmth and color in life which we need. We should say, "I am sorry I have temporarily lost my friend, but I know that he lives. I am not going to mourn, but I am going to think of all the wonderful things he meant to me and I shall treasure the memory of a life well lived and beautifully loved." In this way the sadness can be alleviated. We do not always do that, neither is it easy, because the thought pattern of the weeping of countless generations of heartbreak is behind our tears, and it takes flexibility and faith to turn resolutely from the morbid fear of death to the glorious consciousness of the immediacy of the transition to a larger life.

We should be able to enter into each other's experiences, even the emotional ones, without a negative reaction. We should not reduce ourselves to a place where we say there is no sickness, pain, or suffering, and coldly refuse to respond. Shakespeare penned a great line, which alone should immortalize him, when he wrote: "He jests at scars who never felt a wound." But we must not respond to suffering in the terms of suffering.

There is something in the emotional experience of sympathy,

and of love, and of friendship, which, if we did not enter into, we would miss; not only would we miss it but we would not be complete without it. But if our own emotional reaction is morbid, then it will destroy our mental happiness and our physical health. And so we must learn, in a certain sense, to jump into the water without getting wet. We shall have to have a protection that insulates us from the damaging shocks of human experience. What is it? A faith and conviction so great that it cannot be disturbed, thus tempering our every reaction. A great faith does not take place as an eruption, it does not take place, usually, as a sudden transformation of consciousness. More often than not it is a little here and a little there.

It is scientifically demonstrable that when we fear, when we are discouraged, when we have a sense of failure, a real, definite mental energy is loosed. That is one of the teachings of modern psychology. If discouragement creates a definite energy why would not faith create one? It does, but it travels in a different direction. Fear exudes a certain odor from a person's body which animals sense and which arouses in them a reaction of fear that causes them to attack, in self-defense, the person who is afraid. This principle is scientific, religious, and philosophical. It provides a foundation for the saying: "There is no fear in love; but perfect love casteth out fear. . . . " If we could approach any animal without fear, the animal would not sense fear and would not evidence fear and combat us. That is a whole book of sermons in a nutshell because it validates this teaching of the Bible: " . . . Resist not the devil and he will flee from you." This does not mean that nonresistance is easy. We are all human. But perfect love does cast out fear.

All negation is based on some form of fear. And when we are no longer afraid the experience which was fearful can no longer influence us. We have an intellect which can enable us to so analyze our reactions that we can convert the energy of fear into faith. If that were not so we would be caught in an impossible duality. The *Bhagavad Gita* of India, one of the great spiritual documents of the ages, states that we shall never be able to do this until we do away with the "pairs of opposites." And Jesus put it another way when he said: "Ye cannot serve God and mammon." When our attention is divided, we are divided. We cannot be happy and unhappy at the same time; neither can we walk in two directions at the same time.

We constantly face a changing world. But we seem to long that it might always be static, that it might always be the same, for we do not want to be disturbed from the apathy of our morbidity. It is not easy to shake the shades of unreality from our imagination and look up into the sun, but that is what we must do. We must transmute the energy of doubt into faith. How? By turning the mind away from an idea of isolation to one of inclusion in a greater Whole.

Unless we can find a concept of something bigger than our own littleness we shall ever continue in the confines of our present sense of limitation. It is only as we expose our present morbid experience to the sunshine of the rising Truth, and consciously wed ourselves to a Universe of wholeness and bigness that we shall awake from the nightmare of a life separated from good. It does not matter how long the nightmare may have lasted, when we awake from it it no longer exists.

The Truth overcomes that which is not so — "And ye shall know the truth, and the truth shall make you free." The intellect must decide what is true. In actual practice what shall we do? An experience occurs and it is a happy one, it is constructive. Our entire emotion responds to it with feeling; we know nothing but good, nothing but strength, happiness, and physical healthfulness can come to us. But then comes an experience which causes us to see that our emotional reaction will be a negative one, one of sadness, fear, doubt, or hurt. At once, then, the intellect may step in and say, "I do not wish to react that way. I am not doing it now." There is no other way. We decide how we would like to react to an experience and we have the power to immediately turn our emotional responses into constructive vitalizing channels, creating joyful responses.

There seems to be no way by which this may be accomplished unless we first establish within our own minds an unshaken and unshakable conviction in a Reality greater than ourselves. We must come to see that we are one with the Spirit of God.

We find that if a man fails and accepts a mental image of failure, that very concept will help him to fail again. But if he neutralizes the idea and at once converts its energy into establishing one of success, out of that failure he will create success because he is dealing with a Power and an Energy that makes thoughts become manifest. If a man loses, it does not matter whether it is money, friendship, a business, or his health, and lives in a conviction of the loss, that conviction pushes constructive faith away from him and makes it much harder to recapture. But if his conviction is that he cannot lose, because the Spirit within him cannot lose, then any loss is but a passing experience for the energy of his reaction is favorably channeled. As a man beholds his own countenance in the reflection from a placid pool, so Life frowns or smiles for him depending on the way he first looks at It.

8

MAKE YOUR LIFE WORTHWHILE

*Use the Power
of Your Mind*

In order to make our life worthwhile we first need to define what we mean by Life. Jesus defined it when he said: "Consider the lilies of the field, how they grow; they toil not, neither do they spin: and yet I say unto you, That even Solomon in all his glory was not arrayed like one of these." We do not know how it is that an invisible energy enables the sap to flow up into a tree, or how it is that a chicken comes out of an egg. We may only watch the process. When we say "life" we do not mean merely that which lives, but That by which and through which and in which it lives. That is what we mean when we say Spirit or God — a Divine Presence which has consciousness, power, intelligence, and volition. It is impossible to circumscribe It. We cannot define It too well, but we can feel It. God is a Presence; God is the Law of His own creative action. Love, as the emotion toward self-expression, must dominate the activity of this Intelligence in and around and through Its Law.

We live. There is no argument that can deny our existence, because the very argument that would deny our existence would have to exist and thus announce our existence by denying it. Since we live, that life which we live must be some part of that which is Life, else we could neither live nor be conscious of life. It seems self-evident, then, beyond the necessity of argument, that Life is and that we live. And because, in some slight degree at least, we understand and appreciate and unify with Life, comprehend It slightly and are conscious of each other, we live in a universal Medium. Because we are individuals, we are individualized out of It and from It, but still exist in It and by It. Therefore, our life is Its Life in us, as us. And since Its Life is creative, our life is creative.

The Spirit, out of the prolific possibilities of Itself, does deliver to each one of us individually, and to all of us collectively, as much of Itself, or Its Being, as we at any time are able to accept. When we deal with the creative power of our own spirit we are dealing with the creative Power of the only Spirit that there is. Because there can be only one Life Principle, there can be only one God, therefore there can be only one man — we are all that man.

Thus our nature is such that it is creative. We did not make it so, we cannot change it. All we can do is to use it constructively. Jesus told us to look about us and we will find that we are living in the kingdom of God right now, and to consider the lilies, *how* they grow. They grow because it is their nature to grow, and that nature is God. We live as the lilies live — it is our nature. However, the lily is not self-conscious, therefore it does not block by any volitional act the Divine influx or the Divine outlet. That is our whole problem. The problem is in the only place it could be. We may think the problem is in our business where we are trying to make a living, but it really is in that thing which lives — in ourselves. The business is an effect, and if we shall ever learn how to *live,* making a living will be automatic, we cannot help it.

There is such a thing as spiritual Power in our own soul. No one can deprive us of It but ourselves; however, we can help each other in time of need. When we get temporarily out of adjustment we can secure spiritual help from others to put ourselves right again. But in the long run we must live our own life. We must learn how to live. We must become happy and free in our own mind.

Let us consider this from the standpoint of happiness. We

live now, and when we think we are dying and everybody thinks we are dead, we are going to keep right on living, so why should we not begin to settle the main problems of life here? Why the futile waiting to live? A businessman says he will retire at fifty or sixty or later when he has accumulated whatever fortune he wants to have. He says, "I will retire, and then I will have a good time." He has worked so hard that as soon as he retires he drops dead. People always seem to wait to be happy. They say, "When I get this done I will be happy." No one finds happiness that way. The only man who knows about *living* is the man who *lives,* and somewhere along the line we will have to begin to live spontaneously and creatively *now!*

This does not mean that we should live chaotically, without responsibility or obligation. It merely means that while we do everything intelligently, with the highest degree of integrity and intelligence we have, but do it spontaneously and not quite as seriously as we used to, things will take on a new perspective. It does not matter how big a house we build, someone will build a bigger one. There is no finality to anything. That alone is adequate which satisfies and makes us happy, complete, and secure.

We say God is good, but who says it except the goodness of man proclaiming it? So it seems legitimate that we should desire a betterment of circumstances and a greater good. We should be a thousand times happier than we have been. But we limit the possibility of our happiness to external rather than to internal things. However, we do not want to live in a world of illusion; the external world is very real but it is a passing incident. It is normal and natural that we should enjoy it, but the moment we limit the possibility of our happiness to any particular aspect of it we are unhappy. All the great spiritual geniuses have told us to penetrate first the depths of our own nature, seek that God indwelling our own soul, and know of the creative power of our own spirit through the conscious direction of our thought; then we shall speak our word knowing that it shall be done.

How simple is the method of procedure! What would have happened if the great geniuses of the past had consciously used man's innate ability as we are learning to use it today? They recognized the ability, but they were not living in what we call a scientific age; people in those days did not try to make conscious use of it. Now, for the first time in the history of man, people are consciously and definitely using the creative power of their thought. This means that in addition to trying to think straight at all times we shall take certain periods from the objective duties and pleasures of life to get quiet and create our mental picture of life as we would like to experience it.

We are human and we are going to make mistakes; we are going to say something we should not say, we are going to think something we should not think, we are going to do something that would have been better undone. There is no sin but a mistake and no punishment but an inevitable consequence. This does not mean we can go out and do anything we want, for the Law implies that if we hurt we will be hurt. But we must be flexible with others' mistakes and flexible with our own; we should forgive ourselves everything that we have done that should not have been done, forgive everybody else everything they have done that they should not have done, and know that each shall come to learn the inevitability of Good.

The man who begins to do this finds life will become a continual series of transitions from less to more, from more to much; from good to better, and better to best. There is always the eternal upward spiraling unfoldment of the infinite Possibility through a limitless Principle.

9

YOU CREATE
YOUR EXPERIENCE

*Learn To Do
It Right*

Our individual intelligence has its source in the One Intelligence; however, this does not mean that every act of ours is intelligent. But even the most foolish act of ours would not be possible unless there were an intelligence by which we could commit the foolishness. It has been said that the greatest wrong is the suppositional opposite to the highest good.

One in all sincerity may ask: "If God is all there is, why is there poverty? why is there sickness? why is there pain? why is there unhappiness? Why is it that we can experience negation if God is all there is?" Only because we are *real* beings, immersed in the great Reality. So, if we use a Divine Energy with which to hurt ourselves, and if at the same time we might use that Energy to help ourselves, is this not possible because we are really free? But if we could use It only one way we would not be free. Consequently, it seems that any negative experience in life is bound up in our freedom, and the more we think about this the more we will conclude that the answer to every problem is in the problem. We therefore must try to determine what it is that creates and is having this experience.

Whatever the nature of Life may be, the reaction of each of us to that nature is individual, and, therefore, greatly a thing of our own choice. Two men may go down to the ocean and witness a sunset. One is an artist; to him it is a thing of beauty. The other wants no part of it, shades his eyes and turns away. It is the same sunset, the same ocean, and the same atmosphere, but each takes out of it what he brings to it. Therefore, we arrive at the fact that whatever the nature of the Universe is, Its nature to us is plastic and fluidic, always conforming to our states of consciousness. And we may carry this proposition a step farther: Nothing can exist unless there is something that knows that it exists, either in our mind or the Mind of God.

Why, then, are not our mental attitudes creative of definite conditions? They are. Many persons have damned their environment straight into hell and gone to hell with it, and many of them, after that had happened, began to bless it until their hell became transformed into heaven. There are no devils to us outside our own acceptance and there are no angels to us outside our own acceptance; and even God, in His omnipotence, becomes limited to us by our receptivity to Him. There cannot be an acceptance of anything without a mental equivalent of it.

If we go about cursing — and this does not mean literally damning, but cursing by disapproval, cursing by criticism, cursing by continuous faultfinding — then we are condemning our environment and it shrivels up and becomes distasteful. It is within our ability to select the affirmative viewpoint that gives us the consciousness and the power to change our environment.

Thanksgiving is recognition and praise is affirmation, and life is built out of this recognition and this affirmation. But remember that we may affirm either the negative or the positive. If, because we have experienced evil or lack temporarily, we say, "Well, what's the use? Anybody can see this is what is so," then we begin to affirm the lack and increase the experience of limitation. But if we say, "Good is all there is," and if we bless the good, praise the good, are grateful for the good, and recognize and affirm the good, then we will be creating it.

Now the only way we can demonstrate that this is so is to do it. As we deal with people the silent recognition which we have of them causes them automatically to react to us in the nature of our recognition. We have all seen this happen many times.

For instance, there was a man who needed help. He said, "Where I work the foreman takes particular pains to criticize me; nothing I do is right, everything I do is wrong, and the only reason he keeps me is that I am very valuable to him, but some day he is going to tell me I am through, and I will be glad." This man was told to no longer recognize the criticism but to recognize and praise the Principle of Perfection in the other man. That is not always easy to do. But this man did it, instead of allowing his own critical reaction to arouse and accentuate a corresponding attitude in the other. In a few months the man was promoted and he no longer worked under the foreman because now they were equals. That came about as a result of the spirit of thanksgiving and praise, which is recognition and affirmation.

If we find ourselves in a situation which is unpleasant, we must stop fighting it and antagonizing it; we must begin to praise it and bless it. This is the principle of nonresistance, but it does not mean acquiescence. It means nonantagonistic recognition of the condition, but there is an inner refuting of it because there has been established an affirmation of its opposite. If we are in an undesirable environment, or surrounded by hostile individuals, if we heal ourselves the result will take one of two courses: There will be a change in conditions or a healing of the others' thought about us; or we will be placed in new surroundings. In other words, the logical thought, based upon the nature of Reality, is bound to demonstrate as an actuality. It has to occur, it does occur; otherwise we would just be hypnotizing ourselves and indulging in wishful thinking.

It is of no use to just depart from our environment, because if we did it would follow us wherever we went. There is nothing that can separate us from our own shadows. We cannot run away from anything because what we run from we have created and it runs just as fast as we can — it is like our shadow, it is always right there. We must idealize our job, we must praise it and bless it and see perfection in it; we must see ourselves so expanded that if the job then is not big enough for us we will automatically be lifted into another one. But we cannot accomplish this if we continue to curse, to belittle, to criticize.

We are dealing with the only Intelligence in the universe, and the only Power and the only Presence. It created everything, and It governs all things. But It gives to man the power to have experiences which are like his own evolving thought. We all create our own environment, but according to our own limitations. If we say we are too old, then we are too old; if we say we are too young, then we are too young. Whatever the thought is that denies us our privilege, that is the thought we have to heal. There is nothing to heal but the thought.

Life unfolds from within. I do not know how or why It does it. What difference does the how or the why make? It does it! And if there is such a Principle — and many people have proved that there is — the thing to do it not to argue about It, but to use It; replace every negative idea by creating an affirmative one. Remember that Spirit is never too old nor too young, and Spirit has never failed. We have placed a curse on our experience through our negative thinking. We must bless it, we must praise it, we must mentally enjoy it before we can actually partake of that which we wish to experience.

The Spirit urges us into righteousness, but what does righteousness mean? Right relationship with ourselves, our fellowman, and the Universe. That is what gives birth to truth, to beauty, to peace, to joy, and to power. The Law always reflects the mental attitude, and the mental attitude can be consciously transmuted from one of negation to one of affirmation. There is a unity of Spirit and form, of Mind and matter, hence there is an objective responsiveness in nature equivalent to the thought of man.

If we cannot stop thinking negatively, then we are going to experience negation. It is not that God curses us or condemns us or we are visited with "ill luck." We are blessed or condemned by the act itself. And the moment the mental negation is transmuted into affirmation, not only does it disappear but its tangible

56

manifestation as well. Then we will find we are lifted out of hell and into heaven, which was always there but which we did not see. The worst thing we shall ever encounter or be attacked by is forever our own imagination.

All that is right is delivered to us. The Bible says that we should make known our request with thanksgiving and enter into the gates of Life with praise. The spirit of thanksgiving and praise constitutes an upward thrust of the mind, lightens the burden of thought, heals a sense of oppression and depression. Let us learn to focus our attention only on that in our environment which is worth praising, and forget the rest. Let us learn to be happy even in the midst of unhappiness, to laugh even in the midst of tears, to believe even in the midst of unbelief. The man who does this is the man whose foundation is certain; he is the man whose thought is firmly centered in the invisible Essence of Reality and finally comes to enjoy Its abundance of all good things.

10

YOUR FOUNTAIN
OF YOUTH

*The Years
Don't Count*

Dr. Carl Jung, the great psychiatrist, worked out a very interesting analysis of our psychological nature. He analyzed and described the mental attitudes of the three stages of human experience: youth, middle age, declining age. He advanced the thesis that individuals without a spiritual conviction during the last part of their lives are not nearly as happy as those who have a satisfactory one.

Youth is the grand time of life, and it is the kind of time that should continue, always. The main reason that the young are psychologically better off, and consequently physically better off, is that they are looking forward to and preparing for something else. They are optimistically entering life's race to accomplish; everything is ahead of them and there is no dread of experiences behind them. To be sure, youth is rather callous. Very few young persons think very deeply about abstract problems. For the most part they are carefree, have no physical disabilities, no economic worries, and they have not yet come to experience the so-called disillusionments of life.

The next stage of life, or middle age, is approximately between the ages of twenty-five and fifty. People in this class are busy. They are married; they have children; their whole time and attention is given to their families and to their businesses. They do not have much time to think of anything else. Therefore they generally are, at this age, in a time of fulfillment.

When we come to the third stage we find that so much of life has already taken place. The man of declining age usually has accomplished whatever he is going to accomplish, or he has failed to accomplish it and become disillusioned. He has been in love, he has married and had his children and they are grown. They are now entering the second stage themselves. Unless this man has developed within himself, out of his experience in the two previous stages, a belief which enables him to look forward to something, his mind is continually thrown back upon the personal self, and more often than not he begins to develop physical ailments.

When any part of the body is thought about in a negative way for a period of time something will happen to it. When hope and joy and spontaneity cease to occupy one's thought, the body begins to bog down. The physical disabilities of any age start, in the main, with a mental attitude. When the continuous irritations and agitations of life, with no neutralizing balm to pour over them, persist, diseases begin to develop. They were once mental attitudes but they become functional disorders.

The day that a man has nothing pleasant to look forward to, nothing happy to anticipate, he is lost, and particularly so if he has piled up a lot of negative experience in the past. The one thing that means anything is that *something* which springs spontaneously from the innermost reaches of his consciousness. The moment a man loses that thing, the moment hope goes out of him, he begins to get physically sick and that place in his body where there is the least resistance will be the affected part.

Dr. Jung states that there are two classes of people who pass middle life. In one class are those who do not believe in a future for themselves beyond this life. In the other class are those who do. He says there is no comparison between the two. Consequently, speaking as a scientific man and not as a religionist, he says that a belief in immortality is good medicine, the very best mental hygiene.

The actual belief in immortality helps people who have passed middle age to avoid many of the familiar problems of the later years. This is something worth thinking about, for everyone who is under fifty will be fifty someday and the older we grow the more we are able to realize what is worthwhile. When we were young we thought that money, position, and cleverness were all-important. Later, as we contacted life, we realized that life is from within, that age is not a thing of itself but is merely an accumulation of experiences. If age were a thing of itself and we are immortal beings, we would go on growing older until we were old indeed.

Old age, as such, is a mental attitude, an attitude of depression. Is there anything on earth so pathetic as a man whose spirit is broken and whose contact with life has so disillusioned him that he is crushed by it, through sensitiveness to the rebuffs which he has met? The average individual is only partly happy. If people were never unhappy they would never think of themselves as growing old. They would, of course, grow to be sixty or seventy or eighty, and someday the doctor might say they had died of old age, but they would not — they would have just walked out of this life into another. A person who has enthusiasm for living, who is young mentally, cannot be old for the mind and the spirit are ageless.

It was formerly thought that at a certain age people must become senile. Psychologists and medical men no longer believe that people's mental capabilities have to lessen and deteriorate as they grow older. As age increases the physical movements of the body may slow up a little, so also may the mental processes, but they do not need to deteriorate; instead, they should become a little more accurate, a little more cautious, a little more careful. Therefore, as we get older the mental processes might become a trifle slower, but the mental reactions of the older person should possess more wisdom and judgment than those of the younger one.

The mind is something which we did not make and it cannot be lost. We need to come to think in this way: There is no such thing as your mind and my mind; Mind Itself is, and we use It. There is such a thing as your mentality and my mentality, your personality and individuality and mine, your thought and my thought, but Mind is One and all are unified in It. We all use, as Emerson said, the "one mind common to all individual men." If we can realize this we shall get over any fear of "losing our minds."

Mind *is,* yet because of certain shocks and certain physical disabilities we may appear to lose our minds. But by far the greatest part of all mental ill-health among people who have normal physical bodies is due to mental pressures. A mental strain invariably is the result of a man's inability to unload himself, as it were, into or upon the Infinite.

The man who really believes in a rational and intelligent God more than he believes in anything else will never become mentally unbalanced; he is not even likely to become what we call absent-minded. Absent-mindedness arises out of mental carelessness or mental slumping, a letting go. It is not only the man of advanced years who says, "Well, it is all over now." People of all ages say it. This pathetic condition of inertia, which is quite prevalent, is a great liability. If we lack initiative and expectancy, if seemingly the flame of life has gone out, we are in a sorry state.

I know of but one thing that rekindles the Divine spark of imagination, and that is faith in *something* greater than we are. The only thing that matters is, while we are here are we happy? One man might be happy while he is starving to death, physically. Another man might be unhappy, not because he lacks anything that the world has to give, but because he has not found the only thing that can make any man happy on earth — he has not discovered himself. It is a discovery of the self that makes real living possible. The man who knows that the great, eternal reaches of time and space are his will not worry if he does not happen to have everything that he would like to have today. Neither will he have a sense of loss if something which he thought he possessed today leaves him. Nor will there be any dismay as he walks down the avenues of life.

There is an eternal expansion of the soul. We shall always be more than we are now, and there will never come a time when we shall get through being more than we are or will be. No matter what age we are, we may look forward to the creativeness of our spirit, to the eternal expansion of our own soul. This must be an unwavering conviction. It does not make any difference what we say unless we can believe what we say. There must be a conviction within us born primarily of the Spirit. But it must satisfy the intellect and the emotion. We must be convinced through and through of Reality if it is going to mean anything to us.

Faith, conviction, and belief are real. Spiritual Power is not an illusion, and the world in which we live is the objective counterpart of a spiritual Reality. There is a deeper voice that speaks, beyond the experience, which causes us to know that we are eternal, immortal, and Divine.

Let us forget age and think of life. There are a few simple rules. If we wish to remain young we must never harbor antagonism. That does not mean we are not smart and do not know what is happening. We must be able to know and to differentiate nicely. We must be able to meet the rebuffs of life without being hurt, for it is not the experience but our reaction to it which affects us. We have all had sad experiences, but we must forgive ourselves, enlighten our consciousness, unload the burdens of our thought.

We can all directly experience Reality if we will take the time to do it. We must watch ourselves and not plant negative thoughts. We need to develop a good-natured flexibility. Nature demands this, for if the tree did not bend before the wind it would break. We are apt to hold our thought so static that it finally becomes a habit which destroys not only our mental happiness but also the spiritual influx. Let us try to believe that if God is for us nothing can be against us. Let us live as though today would be our last day, which it might, but at the same time let us live as though we were never going to stop living.

The next world, to you and to me, will be a continuation of this one. Let us, then, look not back with introspective sadness, but, forgiving ourselves the past, put the best we have into life today and look forward with joyful expectation, knowing that wherever we shall be, whatever we shall be doing, that which we are is God. As we come to realize that that which is God is indestructible, ageless Spirit, we shall find ourselves forever partaking of Its essence which continually makes all things new, and knows neither beginning nor end.

LIFE ANALYZED

LAW
Its Power

LOVE
Its Impulse

TRUTH
Its Aim

UNITY
Its Government

INTELLIGENCE
Its Direction

PART THREE

NEW DIMENSIONS OF EXPERIENCE

The mental and emotional wear and tear caused by stress perhaps is created by an apparent inability to resolve the conflicts that arise in your own mind. The wide variance between things as they are and the way you think they should be provides you with a big area of turmoil.

There are sound and workable methods of solution which you can use to alleviate most of your difficulties. You do not need to run away from any problem or blind yourself to its existence. You may so guide and direct your thinking that it rises above any particular involvement and then you can deal with the problem in a logical and coherent manner.

The freedom you desire, the better life, more success, improved health, and harmonious relationships all find their sources within yourself. The new dimensions of living you seek are yours as you expand the dimensions of your thought.

11

THE POWER OF
MIND IN ACTION
*How To Use It
Constructively*

Stripped of narrow, limiting connotations the word *God* can be defined as the intelligent Life Principle in everything, through everything, and around everything. Everything manifests intelligence. The intelligence in the atom we call atomic; the intelligence in the animal we call a simple but largely unconscious intelligence; the intelligence in the human being we call self-consciousness. Then there is the intelligence in those few cases which we call illumined or cosmic intelligence. But all are only different gradations of the same thing. The man who has experienced illumination still uses his other form of intelligence — it is automatically there.

Science tells us of the conservation of energy; that nothing is ever added to or taken from the universe in which we live. There is no more or less energy than there was billions of years ago. The *stuff* — the elemental energy of atoms and molecules — out of which all that has form is made always was, is, and will remain. Yet we know that energy can be converted from one form to another. Electrical energy can be used to produce light, heat, or motive power. Chemistry and physics constantly demonstrate that certain forms of matter can be converted into other forms of matter, but regardless of how we use the energy or what material form it takes, it is always the same elemental *stuff*.

Therefore, we would say that whatever God is, God is not

more and not less than God was. Nothing can change in the Changeless but action and form. Form can change, but the *stuff* which produces form cannot change, neither can the Law by which it becomes form.

It is a sound theory that God-Power was, is, and remains. We also need to recognize that It is always doing something. No form is permanent, but while any particular form may come and go, the eternal Spirit will always be projecting Itself. God will always be creating. The God-Power will always be doing something. But we perceive that It does things in certain places that It does not do in other places. Therefore, we perceive that in God-Power there is what we call selectivity, and selectivity is just another word for freedom, volition, and choice, within the action of Law.

We have, then, an intelligent, initiative, creative Power in the universe always giving new combinations to Itself — through Its own energy and Its own *stuff* — always selecting, forming, and reforming. It is impossible to suppose the initiative of selectivity and creativeness without presupposing imagination. If we were to combine selectivity, creativity, and imagination, and fuse them into one, we would have the abstract Essence of our concrete individual personality, and we would also have what we call infinite Person, or Personalness, the abstract and universal Essence back of and in and through each one of us. This Essence is not something apart from man. If we declare that there is a God-Power in the universe, then it follows that the individual is related to It because he is created by It out of Itself. Inasmuch as this God-Power could not create something unlike Itself, there is inherent in man the potential use of this Power.

What do we discover when we consider natural laws? We have found that even the movement of thought involves electrical energy! Every physical movement implies the action of energy. We also have discovered that every known energy in nature is really resolvable into one eternal Energy which is manifested in many ways. This one Energy may take a particular form, but the form may be converted back again into It. For instance, ages ago the energy of the sun was captured by plants which have become the coal we mine; as it is dug up after countless millions of years and burned it releases the energy and native elements which it contains. All energy is one Energy, even though that Energy takes a million different forms, and that one Energy is indestructible and changeless.

The energy contained in one form, in a last analysis, is the same energy that is in all forms, and whenever intelligent direction, which has established the form or pattern that energy will take, is withdrawn that particular form at once begins to disintegrate. So we find that when the soul severs itself from the body it is evident that the integrating factor has left, because simultaneously with its departure disintegration of the physical body takes place. We may say, theoretically at least, that fundamentally all form is the result of the Self-contemplation of God, and if that Self-contemplation is withdrawn from any particular form, that form will disintegrate but the pattern or idea remains in the Mind of God always, to be manifested in another manner.

If the energy we use is universal Energy, and if the *stuff* from which our bodies and all physical forms are made is universal Stuff, why should it seem strange to say with Emerson that "there is one mind common to all individual men"? It seems logical to conclude that if all form has one Source and all energy has one Source, ultimately all mind is One. Therefore, your body and my body is the Body of God; your energy and my energy is the Energy of God; your mind and my mind is the Mind of God. But what we are is that point in universal Consciousness where we use the Substance, the Energy, and the Mind. That is undoubtedly what Jesus meant when he said: " . . . he that hath seen me hath seen the Father. . . . "

In our daily life we use all types of energy; we use them through conscious, deliberate choice, and with definite direction. But when it comes to the Energy of Mind and Spirit, the God-

Power within us, how are we going to use It? By recognizing that It is in us, It *is* us. All that we are or ever can be is It, as us. In some way which we do not understand but which we may accept, God-Power is the power we use, God-Energy is the energy we use, and God-Mind is the mind we use. Since we exist, and since we have intelligence, and since we use energy and have substance, it is self-evident that we are using God-Power every time we think. We are using the selectivity, the creativity, and the imagination of God with our every thought.

Creative imagination is limitless, having infinite possibilities. The only people who get tired of living are the people who literally have quit living. For if we accept and use our creative imagination there always will be action, there always will be creation, there always will be form and body. Always there will be our evolution and growth. What man will be a million years from now we cannot say, but all we have to know now is how to live in our world today. We need to be fulfilled and happy and free in this world, for the next world will be but a continuation of this one anyway.

We have an innate desire to live, to enjoy living, and to be happy. But to do so we must believe we are going to be happy *today*. Whatever is created as an image of our thought automatically projects itself out of our creative imagination, and by means of Divine Energy, through the mechanical action of immutable Law, there is produced a definite form. We may set the measure into which the nature of God is diffused in our experience.

When God produced an instrument — man — through which God could consciously act, this advent of choice and will enabled man to accomplish that which nature had not done specifically. Our power, our energy, and our imagination is God individualized in us.

We consciously use our God-Power through our creative imagination, but it is our will which decides the direction and the form it will take. The will is not creative, but imagination without will and volition and selectivity is chaotic. Whatever disagreeable things may have arisen in our experience, when we reverse our creative patterns of thought the Law of Mind yields the old forms of thought and takes action on the new, without argument. The Law neither knows nor cares what It is acting upon. And by the same Law which makes men sick they are healed; by the Law that makes men unhappy they are made happy. There is only one final Law in the universe, but we may place ourselves in a different relationship to It. This is through an act of our own selection, volition, and will.

Spiritual mind treatment — prayer — consciously, definitely, and deliberately given, is the spontaneous activity, choice, and will of the unique individualization of infinite Mind in us. The moment that a spiritual mind treatment is given it is being manifested through the automatic action of the Law of Cause and Effect.

This places our own individuality in a different light. Each one of us is a child of God, with a destiny not only Divine but infinite and certain. And somewhere along the line we shall all discover our freedom in and through the very nature of our Source—God. But we shall have no more freedom than we can conceive at any time, and it is always a freedom under Law, never in chaos. Therefore, one who would exercise the Divine creative Power of God for his own success and happiness must not mistake liberty for license and must very carefully destroy in his thought everything that hurts.

In this creative place within us, in this repository of our own thought where we use God-Power, let us learn to experiment. Each day let us establish some new idea for ourselves or some-one else. In the silent contemplation of our own thought, let us affirm our new conviction with enthusiasm and feeling, consciously knowing that our thought, our word, is now the law unto that thing whereunto it is spoken — and then let us accept that it is now fulfilled.

As a result of such use of our God-Power we shall gradually

see appearing out of the confusion of our objective experience a new form, the result of a new idea — the manifestation of a new pattern of thought as a new creation. Gradually we shall be changed from where and what we are to where and what we should like to be. This is a Power which every living soul possesses. But we have to start to make conscious use of It in order to discover a new life.

12

THE ROAD TO
A BETTER LIFE

*It Starts with
an Idea*

For the most part people understand how it is that thought, feeling, and imagination can affect the well-being of their physical bodies, but some cannot comprehend how it is that thought can actually affect their environment. The body seems intimately connected with us; however, the environment does not appear as though it were under our influence, at least to the same degree as the body. A man writing nearly two thousand years ago and discussing a very profound spiritual philosophy — the creative relationship of God and man — stated: "I [Paul] have planted, Apollos watered. . . . " One planted the seed and another watered it, but for completion something else was needed: " . . . God gave the increase."

Suppose someone plants a seed in your garden and you water it. The productivity of the soil will create the plant and increase its number without changing its type. The plant will still maintain the identity and integrity of the pattern which was in the seed. Someone will plant, you will water, tend, and cultivate, but the creative Genius of the soil, the creative Genius of nature — God — will give the increase.

It does not matter whether we call God the Spirit, the Creative Principle of Life, the Intelligence in nature, the Universal Mind, the Divine Mind, the heavenly Father, or something else. One thing we must learn is that it does not matter what we call anything, the only thing that matters is this: Have we the right idea about the thing to which we give a name? Divine Reality responds alike to the symbol of the cross or the crescent. So, whoever plants or whoever waters — in whatever locale, in whatever clime, in whatever period of human history — *something* gives the increase because that is the kind of Life we are immersed in.

Now let us shift the whole idea from the physical realm to what we call the mental or spiritual. We know that a gardener will not get what he wants out of the ground unless he first puts the proper seeds into it. We know that if he consciously plants the seeds, definitely cultivates and waters them, and uproots what is not wanted, he will get a harvest. We can relate this Divine cosmic activity, which we do not control consciously, to our little world of experience, which we would like to control. Let us theoretically do away with the material, physical, or objective universe other than looking upon it as merely a passing show. No one living knows what it is. Strange as it may seem, there is no man on earth who can tell us what the physical universe is because no one knows. But there is no question but that it is something which has form. However, let us say that the whole objective universe is form only — the reflection of a concept, a creation of thought, the imagination of God. Let us, in other words, transpose the whole thing into the realm of idea, for we are living in a mental and spiritual Universe.

We are surrounded by an environment, for we cannot believe, for instance, that any city is an illusion. It is a fact in human experience. The streets, the homes, the buildings, and the automobiles are physical facts. But they are not things of themselves! They are effects, results — things that follow a cause. As we look about our physical environment we may or may not like it. We may think it is beautiful, or we may think it is ugly. We may say it is friendly, or we may say it is unfriendly. But each one's environment is going to be to him, finally, what he is to it.

It does not always seem as though that were true. Someone will say, "I did not think I was going to fail, and yet I have failed." How can we answer that one? This way: We planted our garden and we did not think the weeds would come in, but they came. So we have to pull them out and leave what we planted. Similarly we find that thoughts of failure — subjective beliefs, currents of race belief, the collective unconscious — come up in our experience. Such beliefs carry with them the idea that a certain percentage of people will succeed while others will fail. These are the weeds which we must uproot. We need to eliminate beliefs that we must experience a certain amount of sickness, or a certain amount of unhappiness. These are the misconceptions.

We must always remind ourselves that we are dealing with a Law which is neutral; It produces the weeds along with the good plants. Someone will say, "I do not like to believe that." But there it is! It is not a question of likes and dislikes. It is only a question of what is so and what is not so. We are dealing scientifically with a Power that is gradually coming to be known.

Always goodness overcomes evil; always intelligence can tear up the weeds and leave the rest until finally the plot of ground has no weeds and only the desired plants grow. We permit ourselves to be subject to what the human race believes, to the law of averages, until we individualize ourselves out of it. It does not make a bit of difference how we became involved in undesirable situations, the only thing we really need concern ourselves about is how are we going to get where we want to be. There are many people who spend their whole time analyzing how they got in the sad state they are in but do nothing about it. That is not a good practice. A person who spends his entire time thinking about what is wrong never helps himself to become better, happier, or healthier. We do not discover a joy of living by contemplating sadness.

There is a certain amount of self-analysis necessary, a certain looking into fundamental propositions and problems, to find out what errors we can correct. It is certain that we must proceed into the future on the best the past has to offer, not on the worst. Pessimism is not a spiritual quality, it is a mental disease. Fear and discouragement are the two greatest instruments that any theoretical devil would need to dampen the ardor, enthusiasm, or spontaneity that an individual might have. If we believe there is a Law of Mind, just as there is a physical law of reproductivity, then It can only produce according to the pattern given It.

There is more involved in this than at first appears. For instance, if you do not like me, and I know you do not like me, and I spend all my time thinking why you do not like me, then you will like me less than you previously did. That is why it is that if we enter into a group of people who are having a heated argument, and if we take sides and get mad too, then there is more madness. We all know that is true, and there is a reason for it. It is exactly like throwing gasoline on a bonfire — we are adding fuel to the flames.

We do not control the thought of our race. We do not even seem to be able to control our own thinking, for if we did we would be superior people. But we can at least try to control our thought, and to the degree we can we exert some control over our environment. There is no doubt but that we can fully control it, but do we? Who has yet seen anyone who did it perfectly? However, in such degree as we can shift the basis of our imagery, our belief, our emotional and mental reactions to life, we can come to a place, individually, of peace and security and happiness, then gradually as these changes take place there will be a corresponding change in our environment.

We must reverse every negative process of thought. Suppose we learn to bless and curse not. But someone will say, "I do not curse." Every time we say that our environment is against us we are cursing it, and cursing ourselves in our relationship to it. The principle of love always overcomes hate. Let us bless our environment, visualize it and idealize it in our thought and imagination as we would like it to be. If in our thoughts and prayers we mentally create the conditions we feel will make us happy, that is what will eventually come to be our experience.

All living is from within and never from without. And we have a perfect right to contemplate the kind of environment in which we would like to live. The desired environment should be contemplated in joy, love, appreciation, and recognition. It is impossible for a man to experience the tangible results of his mental concepts if he refuses to receive them. The gift of Life is made, but it must be accepted. So, if we contemplate our environment as not appreciating us, it can only be to us what we think it is. That is bringing ourselves back upon ourselves.

We can only take out of our environment that which is similar to what we give to it. But we may take out more than we put in because God gives the increase. Therefore, each day we should contemplate happiness, joy, peace, love, human interest, wisdom. We should pull out the weeds of thought that come to us implying that nobody appreciates us. We should handle such thoughts specifically by denying them, saying, "Everyone likes me because I like everyone." If we are among people between whom there is animosity, struggle and strife, we should contemplate not the animosity, struggle and strife, but the emergence of the Unity of Good which of necessity has to exist where they are. We need to know that there is One, this One is always a perfect unity, harmonious and constructive; that all discord between these individuals is eliminated and they come together in perfect harmony.

We have this basic principle to work with: There is a unity of God and man. Everything ever made is for the Self-expression of God; and, in our own lives, our experience is created through the self-expression of man. So we must contemplate whatever we wish to accomplish, remembering that there is nothing big or little to the Power that creates everything. Whatever gives us joy, happiness, and peace today, and harms no one, is good; it adds to the sum total of all joy, all harmony, and all wholeness. Let us so unify with our environment that we know we are one with the visible and the Invisible, one with the past, the present, and the future. God does go forth anew into creation through every person who thus identifies himself. Those who have in their thought accomplished this Divine Union have seen through this material world into the spiritual realm of Creativity and Causation back of it.

13

DISCOVER FREEDOM
AND SECURITY

*It's an
Inside Job*

Ever since the dawn of civilization — even ever since the first man arose to his feet and began to grasp the significant fact that he was an individual being in a universe which seemed to be more or less hostile to him — the entire search of the human mind, its whole endeavor, has been to discover and proclaim man's freedom. There has been an innate desire to be free from bondage and the shackles of lack, want, and fear, of superstition and uncertainty, of pain, disease, and poverty, and the fear of the hereafter. Because of this, systems of thought exist — organized philosophies spring up, sciences develop, educational systems are instituted, collective security is sought after, and religions are formulated to relate man to the Power that created him. Living in a world which seems more or less opposed and hostile to him, man feels a necessity to discover that there is a fundamental Good.

The great demand in the world today is for a sense of security, as well as freedom and liberty. But we must be very certain in the experimental stages of testing out what is freedom, what is liberty, that we do not exchange one form of bondage for another. In the religious and philosophical history of the world we discover, almost invariably, that when a group has substituted one kind of religion for another it has not always worked out for the best. The Pilgrim Fathers came to the shores of New England in order to be free to worship God in their own way. But the moment they arrived everybody in the colony found themselves compelled to worship God in the manner that the strong-minded members of the colony decided was the best way to worship God. That was not freedom, not spiritual liberty. It was only freedom from one idea of oppression with another being imposed.

Even in the newer religious concepts of the last hundred years or more, very frequently we encounter people who say that they have found the *real* truth, and then, unfortunately, it turns out that they merely have evolved an idea which they liked and called it the truth. Usually they are egotistical, self-righteous people with an attitude of condemnation toward others. In studying the various systems of thought which have developed in the thousands of years of human history it may be noted how extremely difficult it is for the human mind to conceive of liberty without license and without egotism. We find we can only give birth to real freedom when we have conceived the nature of liberty.

True freedom, true liberty, has something Cosmic behind it. Modern science has stated that we cannot move a piece of paper, which weighs very little, to another place without changing the balance of the entire physical universe. We also have learned that our physical bodies and the stars are made of the same materials. So we have come to the place where physics proclaims that there is such a profound unity in the universe that no such thing as dis-unity can exist. In view of this we can begin to understand what the great spiritual leaders of the past meant when they told us of a greater Unity in which we all live and move and have our being, and that the idea of freedom itself is related with the true concept of the Unity of Good.

If nature and life is one, if God is one — and we know that God must be one for the Universe cannot be divided against Itself — then all is tied together into an indivisible Unity. We shall have to get back to this Unity to find the meaning of freedom. Nothing in any part of the cosmic Whole could be considered as freedom which would destroy the liberty of some other part of It. That would be self-destruction, would it not? So we know that true liberty must spring from this great Unity.

On the other hand, in the manifest universe we see diversity and multiplicity. No two people are alike, no two blades of grass, no two grains of sand, no two flakes of snow, no two drops of water, and yet they are all merged in this eternal and infinite Unity. Therefore, we see that the first principle of Life is Oneness; the first performance of Life is multiplying Itself without dividing Itself. Life must be One and that One, in order to be expressed, must be many; but the many, in order to exist, must live in the One.

We are bound into a supreme Unity; we are tied into an immutable Law of Cause and Effect — that is the way Unity moves into action. Cause and effect is something that happens as a result of the recognition of Unity. Consequently, we are one even while we are many, and since each of us is a part of the Whole, if we seek to destroy each other we only ultimately hurt ourselves. This is the great lesson of Life.

Freedom, then, will come only in such degree as we no longer do anything that hurts anyone, but that does not mean we have to become spiritual or intellectual doormats. I do not believe that God, or creative Principle, wants anyone to suffer for himself or another. How can the Supreme Being desire one's suffering without also experiencing that suffering? And what kind of a God could it be that suffers and imposes suffering in a changeless Reality? Those who think there is a Divine necessity in suffering must have a belief which could only arise out of a theology that is based on morbidity, fear, and superstition, and nothing else.

Still we suffer, but unnecessarily. Why? Because we do not understand. We might say that people suffered darkness until someone discovered how to make fire. They suffered the necessity of transporting themselves by physical effort until mechanical locomotion was developed so that they could travel by steam, automobile, and airplane. We still suffer limitation, not because the Infinite imposes limitation, but because we do not understand our freedom. And when we begin to develop our freedom, which we seldom do directly, we generally create a new bondage. When we kill an old devil we are very likely to give birth to a new and more subtle one. Final freedom will come only as it is tied into Divine Wisdom. What is Divine Wisdom? It can be nothing more nor less profound than this simple proposition: The kingdom of God cannot be divided against itself.

Now, we desire freedom. We do not like limitation, we do not like pain, we do not like poverty, we do not like unhappiness. Why should we? No one likes to go to bed and worry all night and get up tired out in the morning. God does not impose it on us. Why do we do it? Because we sense freedom, we sense liberty, we sense God, we sense *something* in us that knows, but out in the objective world we experience limitation. And the argument is between that which we feel ought to be and that which we encounter in the world of experience. It seems as though we are two people, one who experiences limitation and one who knows there should be none.

What limits us? Anything which denies us our good. If we are hungry and have no food to eat, the lack of that food is a limitation to us. Limitation is not an actual force, an entity; it is but our experience of the lack of good, it is the way we may at this time be experiencing life. Limitation results from a temporary lack of understanding and use of that which is constructive. Consequently, every wrong is just the wrong use of a right, it is the same thing turned wrong side out. A thermometer goes up and down, but it is the same thermometer. So we go up and down the scale from good to limitation; we are playing a tune on the instrument of life, the notes of which are high or low depending on our mental and emotional attitudes as they encompass the constructive or destructive, as they include good or exclude it. All problems of limitation contain their own solutions. If we can see through the problems and reconstruct our use of the Power which produced them, It will create for us what we call good.

The evolution of the concept of freedom in the human mind is a slow process. Many systems of thought which claim to provide liberty only produce new kinds of bondage. We should beware of them. They are born out of a sense of bondage which compels something different to happen, perhaps a grasping after greater life, but leads to increased limitation. If we want freedom we must understand that freedom can never come by the imposition of the will of another. Freedom is born, finally and only, in such degree as some system is devised whereby the individual is allowed complete freedom so long as he does not, in his freedom, impose bondage on someone else.

The aggregate which we call a social system is made up of innumerable units which we call the individual. That is you, that is myself, all of us, and together we make a collective unit. First we will have to get the idea of freedom ourselves before we can give it to anyone else. We do not like that, we wish it were not so. It is much easier to preach than to practice. But we can only give what we have to give. And while we may have, and do have, and must have within us a Divine and perfect freedom, we do not always understand it perfectly. We only can demonstrate freedom as we have come to embody it. Jesus said: " . . . Physician, heal thyself. . . . " In such degree as any one of us gets well, we can heal. If we were well financially but not physically, we would find we could heal where we are well and where we are not well we could only bolster up; however, that would be of help. It stands to reason that light is the only thing that will dissipate darkness — more darkness will not do it.

Any idea which motivates a greater good without limiting the freedom of access to good by everyone tends to clarify thought. As such ideas are first established in the minds of individuals, and then spread to the mass mind, gradually better things will happen and they will happen logically. But this can only begin in that individual unit which we are. If we would like to enjoy freedom from fear, let us heal ourselves of fear. We can do this only by encompassing more love than we have fear. If we would like to heal ourselves of a belief in death, the only way we can know there are no dead people is to know Life; and when we are filled with a realization of Life ideas of death leave us. The moment we get an idea of peace, confusion leaves us. All negations will finally be healed by spiritual realization. That is the only way the kingdom of Truth can come on earth. And just as a little leaven leavens the whole loaf, so will even a little change in our manner of thinking, from the negative to the affirmative, affect the whole course and nature of our everyday life.

14

THE GREATEST OF
ALL POSSIBILITIES

*How To Help Yourself
and Others*

It is but natural, if we feel we understand something which is greatly beneficial to ourselves, that we should also wish to use it to benefit others. It shows that the tendency of human thought is altruistic — that there is more good in us than bad. It has been noticed that the first reaction of most people who discover and try to use the creative power of their thought is a desire to help someone else, some member of their family or a friend. We find a principle involved here which has been simply stated as " . . . he that loseth his life . . . shall find it." In other words, the broader our range of vision, the more it must necessarily include or encompass. If we were to build a high fence around our home we would inevitably shut out a great deal more scenery than we shut in. The largest life is the one that includes the most. As Whitman said, "The gift is most to the giver and comes back most to him." So we find it would be natural that we should desire to help each other.

Everyone desires to have something to believe in, and why not? A person without a belief is like a boat without a rudder in a storm—helpless. When any emergency or negative vicissitude comes into his experience he is shaken because he has not realized *something* inside himself bigger than anything that can happen to him. The soul is immune to negation, triumphant over everything. It is this idea that has constituted the vitality of every religion that has ever come to the world, howsoever crude it may have been.

Now there is a new religious impulse in the world. It appears to be approaching its intellectual apex, and we happen to be fortunate to exist at this time. We seek to take this new concept in all of its purity and beauty and discard all superstitious crudities which may encumber it.

Several years ago one of the leading church denominations of America announced that after six years of investigation their committee—one member of which was a leading medical man—had gone on record as saying that spiritual healing is a reality and must now be accepted. But that is all they did about it! Having announced it, they did nothing about using it. That does us no more good than it would for an electrician to tell us that it is now known that electricity can light our home and we say, "Fine," and let the matter rest. Natural forces, powers, and potentialities must not only be recognized, they must also be consciously used. Of what good is it to say, "God is all there is," unless we understand in some degree that this Allness of God will heal the apparent absence of goodness in some specific and particular area?

Spiritual mind treatment is scientific. It does not deny that people are sick. If they are not sick, for what reason would we be trying to heal them? It is very evident that suffering exists in human experience, but to say that it has to exist is a different thing. There was a time when people did not have radio or television. It was true that they did not have them, but it was not a part of the Law of Reality that they should not have them. The fact of not having them was a result of a state of ignorance—nothing was known about them. In a similar vein it would do us no good to say, "Isn't it marvelous, spiritual mind treatment is possible!" That would be a recognition and acceptance but it would not be a use. We must demand of ourselves that we make practical use of all the knowledge we possess. In the East they have believed in spiritual Absoluteness, spiritual Reality, for thousands of years but they have done nothing about it. The more aggressive West has now begun to make practical use of this knowledge and rapidly advance its application in everyday living.

But what is spiritual Power, and how do we *use* It? It is so simple we overlook It; It is merely the Power of the Spirit loosed by our recognition of It. The attention of the mind upon God, upon Spirit, upon Perfection, necessarily recognizes spiritual Power. It could not be otherwise. But just a recognition of the Power does not do anything in particular for us. The potentialities of that which is abstract and universal will never be specific and concrete until they are channeled in and through a definite mold.

Two relevant statements from the Bible are: " ... things which are seen were not made of things which do appear," and "Remember ye not the former things, neither consider the things of old. Behold, I will do a new thing. ... " What do they mean? What we see comes out of what we do not see; what we see is the result of the invisible made visible. Through a process of faith a person should be able to look where nothing is and through the creation of a mental and spiritual cause there would be the appearance of something as the effect. And by the same process of faith a person faced by an objective obstruction should be able to mentally eliminate its invisible cause and have it dissolve since it would now have nothing to sustain it. This is a perfect teaching. First of all, by a process of faith we can look at emptiness and fill it with something; next, by a process of faith we can reverse the procedure and look at an obstruction which is a physical something and by knowing it is no longer sustained it will be eliminated. That is what all creation is. No creation is permanent; it is the temporary appearance upon and disappearance from the screen of human experience, an objective result of a subjective cause. All subjective causes are invisible, all objective effects are visible results.

Now having recognized this, we must put the Power to use, and this means we must give It specific attention, and not only attention but direction. No force in nature is used without direction. It is only when we discover the possibility and harness it to our definite intentions that the abstract becomes concrete in our experience. We begin to direct the Power by declaring that man is the Substance of God. Man is certainly more than a reflection of God. Man must be the actual Substance of God if God is omnipresent. There is a Real Man; we would not be here if it were not for that Real Man. Within each of us there is a *perfect* man, to which nothing negative ever happened. There is a spiritual idea back of our entire organism. There must be. If our organism is something produced through the process of evolution, then it must be a result of involution because we cannot have an effect without a cause. It appears we are justified in believing that back of every organism there is a perfect prototype, a spiritual equivalent.

In spiritual mind treatment we begin at once to declare that the *reality* of man is God. The Truth about the structure of his body and its circulation, assimilation, and elimination is God; the Truth about him is spiritual; the Truth about him is perfection, which is all-powerful. But there is the obstruction! However, when we look at a physical fact and say it is not a necessity, it will tend to evaporate by the Law of Mind that is comparable to the physical law which determines that when a cube of ice is subjected to a higher temperature that which is solid will become liquid, and when the process is reversed that which is fluid will become solid. When viewed in the proper manner the processes are similar but on different levels. What could be more simple? And yet it is a great metaphysical truth.

All our words have creative power, particularly constructive words. But since we are dealing with the Law of Mind in action, and since thought does direct Its action, it stands to reason that any particular thought in a spiritual mind treatment would only have as much power as we recognize that it has. This is something we do not always fully realize. A spiritual mind treatment is not just an idle repetition of words. Anybody can stand in front of a paralyzed man and say, "Get up and walk!" The words are simple, but would we or would we not be surprised if he got up? And so, added to the words which are necessary, for they provide the channel for the flow of Power, is the consciousness — the thing that taps the Power — back of the words. There must be a great conviction that the words are effective. And the only thing that seems to supply such a conviction is our inner experience and realization of the Divine inherent within us.

When we use spiritual mind treatment for ourselves or another we must remember that the effectiveness of the treatment is not so much in the number of words used as it is in our awareness and consciousness of the meaning of the words. If we say, "God is in this man, and because God is in this man and because God is perfect, there is perfect circulation in this man," the words must have a meaning, a spiritual value, if they are to have that spiritual Power which flows from God. There must come a conviction — and experience will teach one what that conviction is — and in such degree as that conviction comes Power may be distributed to a greater and greater degree. Therefore, a spiritual mind treatment needs to be a conscious act of mind, a movement of thought, for a definite and specific thing.

In a spiritual mind treatment we evaluate the whole situation and resolve it, theoretically at least, into a thing of thought, and heal, remove, or correct the negative causative ideas behind it. We will never be able to heal by entertaining the formative ideas which established the condition as a physical entity to begin with. We will never heal a disease or condition mentally and spiritually without mentally and spiritually rising above a feeling that there is a necessity for it. But how are we going to rise above a sense of necessity for it in our thought unless we say, with conviction, "God is this man and God is not sick"? This is the only possible way. We theoretically translate all things into thoughts and proceed by healing the thought. We need to recognize, as have the spiritually enlightened of the ages, that back of every organism there must be a spiritual or mental prototype which is the invisible and perfect equivalent of the objective manifestation of that organism.

There is always a need to come back to the fundamental proposition that God is the perfect Source of all being; that God is now the only Presence in the physical body, and whatever appears to the contrary is eliminated. We seek to find in our mind an active consciousness of the spiritual equivalent of what one may appear to lack, always feeling that no matter what the negation may be, its direct opposite is an affirmation of that which completely overcomes it, transcends it, and heals it.

We turn to that Divine Presence within, that ever-present Over-Soul which is merged with us, that ever-present Spirit and Intelligence which is ever flowing through us. We seek to know that in the light and the warmth and the power of Its intense Perfection everything unlike It is resolved into its native nothingness; and that there then steps forth the whole, the real, and the true God-intended man, who is perfect.

This is the greatest concept and possibility that has ever been entertained by the mind of man. It becomes to each of us what we make of it. Let us no longer argue whether or not it is so, but, accepting it, let us act as though it were so, and then each of us shall discover that it most certainly is so.

APPENDIX

The Art and Science of Creative Thinking

In giving a spiritual mind treatment or praying effectively we proceed in a definite and scientific manner. It is necessary that we have as our initial premise an absolute conviction that there is a spiritual Law of Mind which molds our thought into tangible form. But back of this intellectual and mental conviction there needs to be added a spiritual conviction equal to it; a spiritual conviction that our world is impulsed by love, governed by reason, controlled through law, and that it is primarily a unity, with harmony and beauty; that there is a Divine urge toward self-expression; and that God Himself is infinite Being creating by Self-pronouncement. The intellectual conviction is one of law and order; the spiritual conviction imbues the world of law and order with warmth and color and emotion.

There is nothing wrong with emotion. The only thing that is ever wrong with it is the way we use it. Any man who seeks to dry up all his emotions is going contrary to the first principle of his own being, which is the inevitable necessity for self-expression — that thing which has propelled him through evolution to the place where he now is. There is an emotional craving for self-expression in every normal human being, therefore it must first exist in the Universe. We know that emotion rightly directed by thought and intelligence is more creative than thought without emotion. Psychological research shows that the best self-expression involves an intense emotional urge for that ex-

90

pression, and that when the emotional urge is constructively loosed into right action it is good; when it is not it produces what we call a neurosis.

So we start with the intellectual and emotional conviction that the manifest universe is a thing of law and order, that it is primarily an expression of Spirit or Mind. The material or physical universe is not an illusion but it is the shape of substance only — real enough but not a thing of itself — for back of every tangible effect there is an invisible thought or form that exactly balances it and is, in reality, its cause. Therefore, back of the objective world there is a mental or spiritual world. The objective world is visible, the spiritual world is invisible. Whenever any given cause is established in the spiritual world it tends to create a physical correspondent in the objective world. Thoughts become things; mental states, aggregations of mental states, become objective conditions.

The next step after absolute conviction is definite intention. It is natural that we should believe that there will be a result to our prayer or spiritual mind treatment else we would not undertake it to begin with. However, too often a definite intention is not included because we may feel that what God wants us to have He will give us. But would we say: "What God wants us to have He will give us, therefore we will not harness electric energy? What God wants us to have He will give us, therefore we will not cultivate the desert? What God wants us to have He will give us, therefore we will not bother to invent an automobile or a steamship or an airplane?" Of course not! We must not feel that this is an endeavor where there is no law and order. The conviction is like setting up machinery to utilize the power in a waterfall; but then we have to have a definite intention of what we are going to do with the power. The Power tapped by prayer may be used in one instance to heal someone; ten minutes later we may use It to make someone happy; the next time It may help someone secure a job.

If we are going to make definite use of the Principle involved we must not only have conviction and intention, but we must use conscious direction — this is the next step. For instance, we capture the energy of the waterfall and we *intend* that it shall light a building. But we *direct* it for the purpose that it may light that building and not the street in front of the building. Likewise, spiritual Energy, unused and undirected, will never produce an actual effect until we specify the effect we wish It to produce. This is where people fail to use the Principle intelligently and scientifically, therefore their results are haphazard, chaotic, spasmodic. In order to make a scientific use of It we must first believe that It is, know exactly what we want to use It for, then state that It is *now* operating in a particular place for a particular purpose or person, at a particular time. Therefore, if we give a spiritual mind treatment for the healing of a physical ailment of someone, that treatment is different, although it is founded on the same Principle, from the kind of treatment we would give if we were treating for someone who wished employment.

The technique of spiritual mind treatment begins with this concept: Perfect God, Perfect Man, Perfect Being. That is the basis of the conviction we must have. The man who needs our help is a part of this Perfect God, Perfect Man, Perfect Being. The only thing wrong with him is a certain experience through which he is passing. There is nothing fundamentally wrong with him; he *is* a Perfect Man. This Perfect Man is what the Scriptures set before us as the Christ in us; that is our sonship of God, the manifestation of God as us, the embodiment of God in us. That is the *truth* about everyone, and it is the revelation of this truth, through the intellect, definitely conceived and consciously spoken for specific purposes, that demonstrates the supremacy of spiritual thought over the apparent — and only apparent — material or physical resistance to man's innate Perfection.

Perfect God, Perfect Man, Perfect Being. We begin to formulate this idea for someone, to direct it, as it were, in behalf of this individual. What are we doing? We are thinking. A treatment is a thing of thought. There is nothing more conscious, more definite, more deliberate than a scientific spiritual mind treatment. It is a specific act of the mind.

In our endeavors we naturally meet this argument in our thought: "Maybe God is perfect, maybe your spiritual being is perfect, maybe the kingdom of heaven is perfect, but look about you at the earth on which you live, and weep." But remember that Jesus said: "Judge not according to the appearance, but judge righteous judgment." The earth and sky do not meet, the railroad tracks do not come together, any horizon is merely the limit of our present vision. And so we must destroy this argument, recognize that it arises out of a false belief. We need to know that there is no lack, no want, no limitation in the Reality of ourselves, and that Reality is a present experience *right now*. We must recognize that any adverse argument to this is neither person, place, nor thing; it has no power, it is not the law of our lives.

Many years ago someone said that he healed a disease by presenting a certain logical argument to Mind, and it was a great mystery to many people. It still is a great mystery to most people, but it is really very simple. We are surrounded by some kind of universal Power greater than we are which receives the impress of our thought and acts upon it. All we have to do is think, because that Power is in us. It is what we think with; It is what we are.

In concluding a spiritual mind treatment, after having refuted the wrong suppositions and built up true ideas, we must believe that it is the law unto the thing whereunto it is spoken. A person who gives a spiritual mind treatment based upon conviction, and having intention and direction, must then believe that something has happened, that the result of his treatment is now making its appearance in the physical world.

So we find the following steps necessary in the actual practice of giving a spiritual mind treatment. We start with conviction: Perfect God, Perfect Man, Perfect Being. We move from conviction to definite intention: "I am now going to use Divine

Power for this particular purpose." Next we move from definite intention to conscious direction: We make the statement specifying the desired result. Then we believe and accept that it has happened and that it will continue to happen, for we have dealt with actual Reality. Anyone who can do this can give successful spiritual mind treatments. That is all one has to know about it, but experience will gradually teach one how to give better and better treatments, how to meet certain arguments, how to handle certain situations, how to heal certain conditions. Naturally one's technique will improve with experience just as in any other science, but one need not wait for some far-off Divine event. That far-off Divine event is transpiring in our consciousness today, in the processes of our own thought as it evolves new ideas which replace ancient concepts. And we know that "new good makes ancient truth uncouth"; we know that with the dawn of a higher consciousness we experience greater good.

Our conviction of love must be greater than our belief in hate, our conviction of life must be greater than our belief in death, our consciousness of abundance greater than the fear — and the experience from which the fear has arisen — of lack, want, and limitation. So each finds — and this is the beginning of the emancipation of the individual — not only that the kingdom of God is at hand, but that the kingdom of God is in him. There is no endeavor in which the human mind may engage which can possibly give to the individual the degree of assurance, of spiritual certainty, that comes from actually demonstrating that as the result of his thought — created by himself in the quiet sanctuary of his own contemplation — there grows in his experience, or in the experience of another, the objective fact which shall prove that his faith is justified through the work which it has performed.

There is nothing more real, tangible, or concrete conceivable than a spiritual idea. To be able to work the apparent miracle of spiritual mind treatment within our own imagination and thought, and know that it provides a fact in our life or in the life of someone else, is the beginning of that knowledge and that wisdom which shall show to each one of us that the Spirit within us is independent of time and space, of circumstance and condition; that It is not conditioned by anything whatsoever, that It is eternal, alive, awake, aware, free, immortal; that each one of us is "a God though in the germ."